The GODyssey with Christ

iUniverse, Inc.

New York   Bloomington

The GODyssey With Christ

iUniverse books may be ordered through booksellers or by contacting:

*iUniverse
1663 Liberty Drive
Bloomington, IN 47403
www.iuniverse.com
1-800-Authors (1-800-288-4677)*

*Because of the dynamic nature of the Internet, any Web addresses or
links contained in this book may have changed since publication and may
no longer be valid.*

*ISBN: 978-1-4401-9018-6 (sc)
ISBN: 978-1-4401-9019-3 (ebk)*

Printed in the United States of America

iUniverse rev. date: 3/23/2010

INTRODUCTION

Welcome to a story that relates to a person whose long series of travels and adventures in life have been performed according to Christ's instructions. The autobiography covers the past 25 years of living the Franciscan Christian life. There are many stories about Saint Francis. They all revolve around his wonderful love for Christ. Brother Masseo , an early Third Order Franciscan, is reported to have asked a rather strange but forthright question of Francis. "I wonder why the whole world comes after you, wanting to see and hear you? You are not handsome, not deeply learned; you are not of noble birth, so why do they come after you? Francis responded; " Why after me? Do you wish to know why? Because God has not found anyone more vile, not more incompetent, not a greater sinner than me. There is not anyone less worthy to do God's work in the world than me. It is so that everyone in the world will know that all the greatness and strength and beauty and wisdom of the world, every virtue and every good is from God not from ourselves." This would assure that there would be no misinterpretation due to the presentation by an influential deliverer. Theoretically there should be no question as to how we should follow Christ. This same principle should be applied to the adventurer of this odyssey. There is no rhyme or reason as to why the author felt chosen. But he is accepting the suggestion to tell his perception of the story. Of course, there are not large numbers of people following him around as with Francis. This does not seem to be a path chosen by citizens of our contemporary society! Yet there are thousands of spiritual people who have incorporated the philosophy of Francis into their own life.

This Franciscan owns nothing and is a servant living in the spiritual desert 24 hours a day. God's action is reflected in every moment. Christ's two celestial principles are love and trust. The love of Christ is of the "agape" nature. This involves sharing love with no return expected. Trust is the extension of Faith. It requires acceptance of events regardless of the results. Both of these virtues are incorporated in almost every activity. The objective of this portrayal is to indicate that the Lord will use any type of person to perform His will if their heart is open.

I am a peaceful, humble , loving male who accepted the call while being the President of my own company. I went from a successful business man to advance intellectually in the Lord's wisdom which led to a "foot washing" servant. Through the years I received many accolades. However there is one that is a tremendously uplifting. It is a "Thank You" note from Saint Mother Teresa of Calcutta. This is a farewell card given to me by Mother when I left Her "Gift of Peace" house. There could not be a more beautiful complement in this world. It is the most beatific praise I could ever receive. It is a relic and a saintly recognition that has supported me for the rest of my life. There are references in this book to Her and the Missionaries of Charities because I was a "live-in" volunteer with them for a year.

The "thank you" note is shown on the next page.

Matt Corbliss, S.F.O.

" Being happy with God means loving as He loves, helping as He helps, giving as He gives, serving as He serves..." (Mother)

Easter 1990.

+
LDM

not lived for others worth living".
Mother Theresa

Happy and Holy Easter,
dear Mat,
with a big, sincere thank you
for all that you've been to us
and our poor. Thank you for
your inspiring example of
generous living for others.
With gratitude, love od
prayers from all of us
in Gift of Peace –
Sr. M. Rochelle M.C, Sr.M. Rambam M.C
Sr. M. Carmel M.C, Sr. M. Dobrilla M.C

I have long thought of writing to my family about my journey through life. Accordingly our individual lives are unique. Articulating my path has given me grace to wonder with awe, joy, and thanksgiving where God has seemed to be leading. I have been able to absorb His requests in my daily relationships. Sometimes when least expected His interruption redirects my life to extreme opposite paths. With each new event there is an indication that Christ is specifically telling us that we ought to be "enabling" other individuals. This allows us to be exposed to the rapture of love, through forgiveness, compassion and physical support. I believe we are required to provide each member of our current audience the ability to share God's love. These principles must be applied even though our general life and its natural law approach does not always coincide with our social laws. As long as I am discussing the human heart of Christ, I would like to describe some of the actions we took based on our understanding of these teachings. I will discuss them throughout the book to show you some interesting opinions. Hopefully then they will relate to the meaningful episodes in our lives that we may live well.

My path seems a natural outgrowth of my childhood, adult experiences and education. This includes an MBA, 16 years of Catholic education, 30 years of raising a family and 25 years living the Gospel. These gave me a framework leading to a cosmic existent view that clarified and expanded over the years. Yet, my path seems a bit unusual in comparison to many in our society. I have been professed as a Catholic Secular Franciscan, (formally the Third Order of St. Francis), in 1953.

That placed me in a community allowing the ecumenist principles independent from bureaucratic control. It gave me unforgettable experiences in love and life that can be reflected in my elder years.

I can't help but think that the Franciscans are fulfilling the needs for many of the downtrodden individuals throughout life. This produces a great influence to our world at large. That is for others to review, but for me I believe that I have had the greatest of lives. Some intellectuals could see it as a contemporary disaster in our materially oriented society.

Christ's celestial message is specifically telling us that we ought to be "expanding" other individuals with true love. They are to be exposed to the rapture of love, through compassion, with forgiveness. When physical support is required it must be given also. Doing this is a way of living the rewarding good news of the Gospel. My reflections in the following chapters describe some of these actions. My mature morality is based on my understanding of a way to apply Christ's instructions for living the Gospel. Hopefully, you can relate to the meaningful episodes in my life to your own insights and experiences. I am presenting issues that have developed in my intellect and I feel they should be viewed in the manner presented by Christ. It is intended to prepare us for another level of love after we leave this world.

The Community of St. Francis was not founded as a different path to God (through Christ to us). It was founded as a conduit through which God's love can flow anywhere. The number of persons who have benefited from this river of Love is well in the thousands. The seepage of love does not require the following of a certain set of rules or way of life. The Community nurtures all life given by God for the good of their neighbors and the world. There is a quote from Mother Teresa of Calcutta that is precisely related to the Community of St. Francis 'The Lord does not demand us to be successful in life, just to be Faithful"

There are many other items that put me in a condition that I can spread the love of Christ through St. Francis. My primary position is to help persons afflicted with AIDS. The secondary effort is to help any poor individual who needs love, compassion and support. Let us pray that we will each and all find our way and perform it well.

LORD, make me an instrument of your peace,

that where there is hatred I may bring Love,

where there is wrong I may bring the spirit of forgiveness;

where there is discord / harmony,

where there is error / truth;

where there is doubt / faith;

where there is despair / hope;

where there is darkness/ light;

where there is sadness / joy

LORD grant that I may seek rather to comfort than to be comforted, to understand then to be understood, to love then to be loved, for it is by forgetting one's self that one finds, by forgiving that one is forgiven, and it is by dying that one awakens to eternal life.

The above is an up-dated version of the Prayer of St. Francis .

THE COMMUNITY OF ST. FRANCIS

The Community of St. Francis was founded in Caroline County MD in 1987. It was founded as an institution through which God's love could flow. It was a refuge for individuals who were HIV infected. The homeless needed assistance in survival and dignity in dying. These streams produced by the loving river provides the inspirational flow to the Kingdom of Heaven. The flow of love does not require the following of a certain set of rules or way of life. The Community of St. Francis nurtured all life given by God for the good of their neighbors and the world (Mt 5 38:45).

This book is offered as an overview of a life's journey, focusing primarily on the years of working with the marginalized individuals in our culture. It is being presented to show how the Holy Spirit can work in all of us regardless of our position or state in life.

Along the way, much of the recognition and direction came through prayer, but there was also recognition, advice and support from others. This supported the ongoing possibility of the Community and my own way of being.

I was an AIDS caregiver for more than 20 years. This ministry started, after an amicably separation from my wife. Our seven grown children were out on their own. I was also a live-in servant in a Catholic Worker house in Washington, DC. for one year. I went to Dorchester County in 1991.There I established a hospitality house for persons with AIDS. It became The Community of St. Francis. The home was dedicated to those persons, who are at the end stages of their life. The arena involved the time and service to individuals who were between the hospital and the grave. The intention was to provide a home environment with compassion, understanding, and love. The daily routine became normal house keeping, meals , shelter and transportation. If there were bedridden Guests then medical requirements and paramedical tasks were included. The greatest benefit of the ministry was not that you were there with compassion and understanding that could touch the Guests, but it was to have their aura touch your soul. It becomes very significant when their pain became your pain and their peace became your peace through your loving spirit. Dignity and respect are the most important elements of these services. The approach to those with the HIV virus has been described as "Heaven In View"! Each HIV sufferer was given the opportunity to express his/her views and be listened to regardless of the subject. It all boils down to "living with AIDS and dying with dignity". Over time, the arena was expanded to others with different types of fatal diseases, such as Huntington's disease and cancer. The Community of St. Francis provided a path to Christ for fifty seven (57) souls who left this world in a loving and peaceful atmosphere. As the effectiveness of medicine became more positive prolonging the life and quality of life, especially of those with AIDS, we expanded our mission to include homeless individuals with any serious illness. The greatest number of homeless came with mental disorders. The population became mainly those who were socially marginalized (homeless, addicts, ex-convicts and minorities) with no resources or support. This indicates that all persons were welcome, regardless of race, creed, background or sexual orientation.

My 24-hour services continued, but along the way there were times when volunteers would appear for a while. We began to head up an effort to provide the non resident homeless with food (in the house and the St. Anthony pantry) and shelter. We expanded to two houses. There were men, women, and children visiting the Community of St. Francis daily. They needed a variety of things but. mostly food and money. If we did not have an empty room available, we would put them in a hotel. We often worked with professional social workers in service to those with serious problems in the county, We, the COSF workers, were all volunteers. We considered ourselves a small Christian community/ organization assisting individuals in need, eventually with a personal crisis of any kind. We were friends serving friends as Christ has taught us. This dictates that we must be compassionate, loving and understanding to "the Jesus in front of us". Ours was a giving, caring, and loving relationship with those we served. We felt it imperative to show our Guests respect and retain their respect for us. We hoped to enable/empower, by love, caring, and service, the grace of a peaceful death or, if possible, the return to being as productive in society as their talents and abilities allowed.

Another recognition of the outstanding performance is being selected the:

National Outstanding AIDS Caregiver
1995

The award was granted to the author by the Mary Fisher's Family Network .One of his nominators quoted "He has been a Godsend for us, especially when the care of a patient has tried the limits of us all. He stands as an advocate for the patient and the right to die with dignity".

He was selected as the 1995 Outstanding Caregiver based on his effort running The Community of St. Francis Hospitality Houses on his own.

Matt Corbliss, S.F.O.

The Daily Banner/Tom Russo

AIDS Foundation receives funding

Matt Corbliss, left, received the Outstanding Caregivers Award from the Family AIDS Network at Friday's meeting of the local AIDS Foundation. Mr. Corbliss is holding the plaque that comes with the award, Patricia Finley, president of the local foundation, is holding the $15,000 check that will help fund the two St. Francis homes here, where AIDS patients are cared for. One house is in Church Creek, the other is in Cambridge.

The Daily Banner — Monday, October 23, 1995 – 11

Dorchester County man wins national AIDS award

LOS ANGELES — Mary Fisher announced today that a Dorchester County Secular Franciscan brother has received a national award from Mary Fisher's Family AIDS Network. Brother Matthew Corbliss, founder of the Dorchester County AIDS Foundation, was chosen for one of the group's eight 1995 Outstanding Caregiver Awards. The awards recognize AIDS caregivers for unusually long and dedicated service.

Brother Matthew was one of eight winners chosen from more than 100 nominations by a national panel of AIDS experts.

Brother Matthew has founded two three-bed homes for people in the end stages of AIDS and is cur-

rently the only caregiver in one of the homes. He is working to develop a third house, for women with children. In addition to his caregiving, he is active in support groups, advocacy for people with AIDS, and speaks regularly on AIDS education.

As one of his nominating supporters wrote, "He has been a Godsend for us, especially when the care of a patient has tried the limits of us all. He stands as an advocate for the patient and the right for each to die with dignity."

The Award includes a $15,000 cash grant to the Dorchester County AIDS Foundation to implement a Caregiver Support Plan submitted with the nomination.

The funds will be used to develop both volunteer and paid respite workers to reduce the strain on caregivers in the homes funded by the Foundation.

The Family AIDS Network was founded by artist and activist Mary Fisher, who long has focused keen attention on the important role of caregivers in response to HIV/AIDS.

It exists to fight HIV/AIDS by transforming concern and awareness into effective action and compassionate commitment. Ms. Fisher, whose work was recently exhibited on Capitol Hill, tours the country to encourage AIDS prevention and cheer on HIV/AIDS caregivers. She is an HIV+ mother of two sons.

Chapter 1
THE BEGINNING OF
THE END

There was a scream coming from my boss as he came running down the street from our tool shed that was located in the basement of the office building. As he reached me I could see his face was stricken with fear. He grabbed my coat collar and screamed "don't go down there". His grip on my coat was so tight that when he let go of my coat I wound up on the ground. He kept yelling and continued to run. Of course I didn't pay attention and continued on. I started down the steps and I saw two people curled up at the entrance. This was not unusual because it was warm, and people spent the night curled up. I yelled at them and wondered why my supervisor was so upset. I leaned down and shook the shoulder of the closest one. His head fell forward and there was blood all down his back. There were two dead bodies at the bottom of the steps. They were executed with bullets in the back of their heads. There was blood all over the place and bruises on their heads. I did not realize at this time that my mission was going to be dealing with death on all levels. This would be the least burdensome posture when all we had to do is identify the person and bury their bodies . The neighbors accused me of being involved because I was there. The police didn't even bother to question me. These were not just housing problems. The social problems were primarily dealing with drugs. My future would be smothered with the ill effects of the drug culture including violence.

Sorsum Corda is a development of houses in down town Washington D, C. It was built   with the support of the Archdiocese to provide housing for low income families.. It was past the anticipated age of the initial housing material., therefore, the neighborhood was in need of severe maintenance. This is why I was there as you will see later. For now, lets finish this short scene.

It was not unusual to be walking across the courtyard and hear gunshots, primarily from automatic rifles. What you basically had to do was stop momentarily, make sure you didn't get hit with a bullet and then casually continue walking. Then there could be a woman come to her back door with a shotgun in her hand and asking the question. "What is a white man doing in my back yard". Eventually I was accepted, in the neighborhood, but most of the people thought I was an undercover cop. In Washington, DC the police force had a special group of that kind called the "jump out" team which consisted of a white male and a black male in an unmarked car .They would patrol the neighborhood and respond to bad situations immediately. They were not very popular. I was not too concerned about that, until a few weeks later, I came to work in the morning and the house that nuns lived in had two bullet holes in their front door. The police suggested that I not continue working there because the residents are convinced I was a JO cop and might decide to get even. I stopped working for my health but it was a preview of my involvement in deaths overbearing demands in the future. This was an eye opener. Serving and living with the down trodden added a new dimension to my life.

The key to me being in this situation was a "coming of attraction". The presence of death is due to an intriguing suggestion from the Lord. The eventual life encounters included both spiritual and physical departure. There were hundreds of persons who left this world to be with the Lord with the loving fragrance of the Community of Saint Francis.

The new career started when I was in my fiftieth year. I was in my apartment attempting to meditate precisely on what the Lord wanted. He showed up to let me know His anticipation. It is following Christ's message to it's complete fullness.

Let us start at the beginning.

Lord, there is no fear. I had everything wrapped up nice and neat. Now you want to renege? (swish) What was that? "The sound of the sledge hammer I use to get some peoples attention." O.k. Lord, you have my full attention. Through out my life while serving my family and helping people I always heard a whisper "You are here to serve". Now you are shouting loud and clear. "you are here to serve". I Got it?" Yes, but (hesitation, warning, don't say it) how? BINGO! It's all over. "Here's how!"

"First, work for Me full time, not eight hours a day. "O.k." Second, forget about joining the hierarchy i.e.

Brothers, Priests, Become a true Secular Franciscan! "O.k." Third, sell everything and give it to the poor! "Hold up Lord, you've got to be kidding, right?" (swish) "Fourth, no more sex! "Forget it, I could never be that good, I love sex! Hello are you still there? How come no swish - BONK - "Ouch!" Have I gotten your attention? "Yes" well?" "O.k. but I'll need a lot of help." You've got it.

If you think I was shocked you should have seen the look on my pretty carpool friend's face when I told her. First she laughed, then got serious and said, "we'll see." I felt the same , we'll see. That was 25 years ago and the Lord is still helping and my carpool friend is still in my life. The Lord means it when he says the help will be there when I need it. I still need a lot of help and I still love sex. The love of the Lord is amazing. Again, I am not attempting to elevate myself by this admission. It is important that the world sees that even a lowly person (a drunken, sex addict) like myself can achieve unbelievable height with the help of the Lord. Of all the miracles I have seen, I believe this is the greatest.

I gave up my job and went to work for the church. I have an M.B.A., years of teaching experience, youth ministry, CCD all of those things. Surely any parish would love to have me, right? WRONG. Resumes went out, nothing came back. Alright, I must be doing something wrong. I'm an expert on writing resumes (maybe I should try writing in Latin)? Let's go talk to our pastor Rev. Bob Duggan.

"Well Matt, it seems you don't have the proper degrees for parish work, but I do have a solution. We have a position called Ministerial Intern. It is like a management intern in business except you will learn to run a parish. Your computer background will be very helpful to us." I still don't know if this wasn't a Bob make up. He is such a nice guy that I think he didn't want me to lose my enthusiasm. It worked. Bob insisted on paying a salary which I did not need. Life was great, I lived five minutes from work which was enjoyable and I got paid. Who could ask for anything more?

ST. ROSE OF LIMA

You know who was not satisfied - the old sledge swinger. It seemed this job was too easy to fill the requirement for getting closer to the Lord. Yup, it was. Some months later I read an article in the Washington Post about Michael Kirwan, who ran a Catholic Worker house in Washington, DC. He was by himself and not only housed the homeless, but also bought food to persons living on the "grates." (Swish), I decided to meet the man and see what the possibilities were for me to join him. This tested my patience and persistence. After months of trying, I finally got together with Michael. I definitely got the impression that he was discouraging me. Disappointed, I went home.

"Matt, there is a Sr. Roach on the phone asking to speak to you. She is talking about a Housing Project Maintenance job (using tools). I think she has the wrong number." This was Sr. Rose, who was on the staff at St Rose Of Lima parish. We worked together and I sort of agreed with her that building maintenance was not my thing.

"Hi, I'm Diane Roche, and I understand you are moving into the Catholic Worker house with Michael

Kirwan. He also tells me you're handy with tools. I am the Resident Director at Sursum Corda and we are in desperate need for maintenance help. Can you help us? " "Well Diane, I didn't know I was moving into the Catholic Worker house. Yes, I am handy with tools, but by no means a professional maintenance man. I have an office job here at St Rose of Lima. All that is left is to hang-up. (Swish)

Sr. Diane has a melody in her voice and sparkle in her eyes. You just don't refuse this woman anything. She simply said "So what, we need you. Can you come in tomorrow?" O.k.   She is working at Sursum Corda. As mentioned before, it is a low income project geared to allow persons with limited income to purchase their own home. The complex is actually well planned and had nice houses. It was 20 years old. The expected life for the materials used seemed to be 20 years. The plumbing was atrocious, the structures were abused and there were many abandoned houses that were in ruin. Sr. Diane had me fill out an employment form (the complex was run by a management firm) and asked me when I could start work. My apartment was about 25 miles away and Michael Kirwan was difficult to contact. I explained this but little Miss Perky was oblivious to this and asked me to report to work at 7:00 the following morning. It was winter. The central heating system has broken down and there were growing problems everywhere. We had to repair plumbing, without shutting of the water, because the shutoff valves did not work. The only way we could stop the water was to shut of the whole block at one time. Needless to say in the middle of winter,, this was a horrendous condition. The maintenance crew consisted of two men, one a professional and me. We had a tool shed in the basement of the main office. It was frequently broken into. That is why I didn't get upset when I saw the two dead men. I thought they were sleeping. This naiveté was the beginning of the Odyssey

At this time I felt that another way to discipline my spirit and reduce the cost of my upkeep was not to eat meat. The primary reason was to deny myself one of my other sensory pleasures, but it also made me a "cheap date". I felt that this would also help with the food available for the guests at the Catholic Worker. This was not a factor. Thanks to the good work of Michael and the generous benefactors there was a fairly well balanced menu provided for the people at the house and often for those on the office building heating system grates. The biggest problem was how to transport the food .

In the year I worked at the Catholic Worker, we accomplished a great deal. A gentleman came from Ohio with farm equipment to the West Virginia farms and produced marvelous crops. The interior of the house was painted (thanks to another guest named Matt). Very expensive windows were donated and installed while the men at the house helped frame them. We got some persons in programs for their benefit, mostly antibuse for alcoholics. There were major challenges in discipline and physical protection of the house and the people living there. Drugs and drunkenness were the biggest problems because these persons would be a danger to themselves or cause turmoil for others. The Catholic Worker House was situated on 13th and T streets. The back yard opened on to a street like trail known as " drug alley". It was so active that we would have the police cars, helicopters and gunshots interfering with the nights sleep. Fortunately we had no major injuries and most of the guests at the house accepted the rules and the discipline graciously. It was a period of rapid spiritual growth and maturity for the servant.

Midway into my stay at the Catholic Worker, I became friends with a nice guy named James. I would be remiss not to mention my favorite friend and master panhandler David Allen Kidd III. He was a genuinely good person with a tremendous drinking problem and the ability to con money out of anyone even my daughters. He was also capable of pan handling $20 bills outside of

Mickey D's in Washington, DC. He fought hard and at one point stayed sober for four months on Antibuse. He didn't understand that alcoholism is forever. This fostered a decision were he felt he was cured and wanted me to know. He was so convinced he was cured, that he had a friend record in a tablet pad his reaction as he took each drink. He also gave his friend a drink after each second drink. The history ended with unreadable scribbling off the end of the pad and the two historians off the edge of the curb in the street. "The Kid" was prophetic. He told me I would have a house someday and asked if he could live in it. Unfortunately, he was up at the farm where he hated, but, would go to dry out. He was struck by lightening.

Back to James. He was ill. He had a difficult time going through agencies to get help. If your homeless and can't pay, you are sometimes ignored or mistreated. Unfortunately one day he went to Social Services and waited seven and a half hours. The next morning I went down with him. We signed in at eight o'clock and we sat in the reception area. At 8:30 I just happened to notice two women going up the stairway with breakfast in a box. Around five minutes to ten I had to put money in the parking meter. As I went by the receptionists desk, I stopped to read the headlines on the Washington Post. The receptionist picked up the phone and said. "James has a white guy with him who looks like he could cause trouble. You had better get down here. " By the time I returned James was in the Case Manager's office with the request for medical help. He became so sick that I took him to the emergency room at Howard University hospital. The following derogatory remark should be tempered by the fact that there were literally fifty people in the ER. It was Standing Room Only. James was diagnosed as having liver cancer. He sat in a wheel chair for 3 days and nights suffering. I was furious and demanded action. A very nice, but obviously badgered social worker gave me an address, 2800 Otis St, Washington DC. She patiently explained that they had no beds open in the hospital and no nursing homes to take James. If I took him to that address, he would be taken care of. She would not tell me who or what was at this address. I had no choice. We drove to the address . The building sat on the top of a hill separated from the rest of the neighborhood and had the appearance of a school. It turns out it was once an orphanage.

There was quite a bit of land surrounding the building and landscaping was very neatly maintained. Being on a steep hill it required a classic driveway. The entrance was an artistically structured overhead protection. The building was made of brick, was five stories high and had around 25 bedrooms. Each floor had a multiple function bathroom. There were four showers, two tubs along with four toilets and four sinks. Based on the overall atmosphere these people accepted what they were fortunate enough to get and had no complaints about the lack of privacy. The building was divided into four sections. The first section was dedicated to homeless men. The second section is dedicated to individuals who were sick with any transmittable disease. The third was personal problems involving HIV/AIDS. This section was not to be made public at this time, very little was known about this virus. The fourth section was for women only and there were only four beds available.

Generally it was not the best of circumstances. This is a problem that continued to follow me for the full 20 years. It is difficult for people to understand the danger of a woman being in a shelter. Even one run by Mother Teresa. Women were accepted regardless of what their problems were. There was another section in the back. It was for the Missionaries of Charities novitiate. I had no idea what this section consisted of . I only know that there were times when the chapel would be taken up by the sisters. They had a second chapel in the building that was similar to a small church. The small one was the daily chapel. When Mother Teresa came to be with this group we would have mass in the larger chapel . The Lord gave me a reward. How? By allowing the large chapel to be directly across the hall from my room. This was greatly appreciated for beginning intimate prayer routines.

We pulled up to the front door and immediately a woman dressed in a white sari with blue trim came to greet us. She had a Slavic accent. She immediately went to help James out of the car (no small talk). Her first words shocked me with their seeming insensitivity. She said, "Oh goot, you can walk, we have many who cannot." I thought "and a good day to you too, sister". This wonderful disciple of Mother Theresa's was known as Sr. Dobrilla. She was and hopefully still is the most sensitive, loving, compassionate person I've ever known. Her manner is abrupt and no nonsense because that is the way things are. Her greeting to James was a fact, no sugar coating. That is her nature. That matter of fact nature was for business only. Once the circumstances demanded compassion and love, she was gentle and concerned doing whatever was necessary to make the person in need comfortable and loved. Much of my current actions involving those at the end of their stay here on Earth were learned from this woman. Often she was torn between attending a dying person and obedience to the call to prayer. This would not be a problem here because the greatest prayer is to serve the Christ in front of you.

After James settled into his room I could see that he would be bedridden, so I suggested to Sister that I would like to come each morning and take care of him. There were about 15 others in the section with James and I could see that caring for James would be a burden. (Swish) I did this. Within a week, I was also helping with the showers, baths and cleaning the rooms of the other people. This went on for months. Basically, I devoted the mornings, starting with 7:00 am Mass, to the Gift of Peace (the official name for 2800 Otis St.) and the afternoons and evening to the Catholic Worker. This process brought me in contact with many wonderful Sisters plus the members of the Catholic Worker movement.

Taking care of James introduced me to the beauty and splendor of sharing love with other persons. His disease had progressed to the point that he was near death. It was getting close to noon one day so I was trying to help him eat. In absolute silence eight nuns came into the room. One of the most beautiful things I have ever been exposed to is the Missionaries of Charity choir. Sister Dabrilla had the group sing a few hymns then ask James if he would like to request one. He was obviously weak but requested "Amazing Grace" The sisters started beautifully and James joined whispering. There was a wonderful aura present in the room. There was a radiance around James. The rest of us were full of Love. A t the end of the third verse James , who was lying on his back, lifted his arms half way. The glow became brighter and he sat up half way. His voice was over powering.. In my mind he looked like Moses with flowing silver hair, an earth shattering smile and an invitation to home. He looked up to heaven as if anticipating a hug. He closed his eyes fell back and he was with the Lord. Sister told me to take care of him. I sat in the bedroom for an hour just to be in that contemplative state.

The year progressed well. The Catholic Worker house was running smoothly and at Gift of Peace, somehow I was not only helping with the homeless, I was also helping with another section. The one that was reserved for persons with AIDS. I knew very little about this disease, but soon educated myself. The simple methods of protection, rubber gloves and special apron used by the Sisters are still in practice today. Many people have asked me "when did you decide to take care of people with AIDS?" I never made a conscious decision. Something had to be done and Sr. Dobrella would say "Maatty, we need to do this or that," and we did it.

What a great series of events that were directly in line with the Franciscan charisma. All the beds were occupied, the house was pleasing in hospitality and every thing was doing well. There were a few vibes being felt but not predominant. The "left fielder" (a Joisey description of a person who can change the game with one play) only had the ball in his hand. This is a background program.

(Flash Back)

When I was working at St. Rose of Lima, my coworker Sister Rose acknowledged that I did not fit in the position our pastor had given to me. She took the initiative and arranged to have lunch with Father Joe Nangle who lived in a Secular Franciscan Community known as the Assisi House. Father Joe told me they are looking for an individual to come into the house who did not have to contribute money but would perform political actions related to government activities. He saw the possibility that I could join them. However, I had to point out that I was in the middle of negotiations with Michael Kirwin. Therefore, I could not make a commitment. You may remember that Mike was difficult to meet with. I finally got with him and his attitude was laced with discouragement. I called Fr. Joe to tell him that my decision would be in his favor. Unfortunately he told me that they had selected a Franciscan Brother from another organization. His name was Brother Vianni . Okay, that was no problem. One week later I was accepted by the Catholic Worker. Thanks to the " left fielder" Sister Diane.

Months went by, and I started to help at Gift of Peace. I noticed there was a real nice gentleman, who was the epitome of the fourth vow taken by the Missionaries Of Charity which is cheerfulness. He was most pleasant to be around, and he would perform any action the Sisters would ask him to do. When I went over to introduced myself he was manicuring toes on a street person. They were horrible. I was absolutely shocked when he indicated that he was living at the Assisi house. He and Fr. Joe are friends. He is Brother Vianni. He had become my replacement. Rather than a replacement, he will become a very important sojourner in my challenging path. End of Flashback

Having spent almost a year, I mentioned to Michael that I would like to go on a retreat. He knew of one somewhere in Pennsylvania. Who would ever think of going to Pittsburgh, PA to have a joyous retreat?" The jokes went on "of course it's a silent retreat, how can Matt keep his big mouth shut? Who in PA is not a thief? Every one I know claims to be a "stealer". It was mid September and a good time for a retreat. My anniversary at the Catholic Worker was coming up and it was time to reflect. Michael knew a nun in Pittsburgh, who was administrator for this retreat. We wrote to her and I was accepted as a scholarship attendee. As usual, there was a reluctance on my part to give up the week and go to Pittsburgh. There was also a question whether or not I could keep my big mouth shut for a week. You could not have ordered a more perfect site or weather for anything but especially a retreat. The sun was shining every day. Mother Nature was begrudgingly allowing the iridescent twilight colored leaves to embark on their windblown journey. It was as if she knew the necessity of affording the beauty of creation as a confirmation of spiritual sojourn. It was the most peaceful and enlightening retreat I have ever attended or given . I was in union with the Lord. Ah, peace. Returning to 13th & T Street there were some surprises. There is no value to enumerating all of them here. Suffice it to say that most of the meaningful things we had worked on seemed to have been reversed in one week. Such as people being drunk, some sleeping on the table and others searching other peoples rooms. I found out later that someone had stolen my tape-recorder. This quickly eliminated the "high" left over from Pittsburgh.

Prayer was in order, but some medicine had to be picked up at the Municipal Health Center. The Health Center was on a street that was a direct line to Otis Street. Knowing the Gift of Peace needed live-in volunteers, the thought to go there had been floating around in the back of my mind. This was a Friday and for some reason there was a three day weekend. This stands out because in my mind Tuesday would be the day of action. It is now around 2 O' Clock and I am sitting in the car, after picking up the medicine. The usual mental gymnastics started. What should I do? Is leaving the Catholic Worker a good idea? Is it what the Lord wants? About this time there was a definite impression (I never say I hear voices because my friends in the psychiatric field would lock me up) that said, 'go see Sr. Rochelle, Now!" My response was "O.k., I'll go see her on Tuesday." The impression preceded by a SWISH, was much louder and the comment was "I SAID NOW!" The rest of the afternoon was spent with Sr. Rochelle reviewing the rules of being a volunteer and the fact that having a computer in my room was out of the question. I moved in the following week.

My year at Gift of Peace was exciting because I had entered the semi-regimen of a religious order. The volunteers didn't follow the same schedule as the novices, but we did start the day with Mass and worked until 1:00 pm. Theoretically, we were to get two hours to rest in the afternoon. We were due back at 3:00 pm through dinner. Our dinner time was usually around 7:00 pm. We either had what was left over from the guests meals or foraged for our food in the refrigerator. It was easy to fast.

There were two incidents involving "Eddy" and "Johnny". Eddy was 23 years old and a very gentle and courteous person. He had two huge ulcers on his buttocks. One on each cheek the size of a saucer. Needless to say any excrement would be extremely painful. When something did happen, he would alert us by yelling frantically (I didn't blame him). Not only did you have to change his diaper, but also the bandages. This was excruciating. I can't say he took everything with a smile, but it was close. He only asked us to be gentle. He was a wonderful example of loving tolerance of pain. I was honored by his asking me to instruct him in the Catholic Religion. He eventually was Baptized and he selected me to be his God Father. He passed away peacefully with his favorite person at his side, Sr. Dobrella. I was second on his list.

Johnny was different. He was caring and gentle, but his favorite pastime was watching the look on the Sister's faces when he showed them his picture dressed in "drag "with the white rabbit jacket that he was to be buried in. My poignant memories of Johnny were not only as a friend, but of an individual through whom I was convinced I could not contract AIDS in any manor other than those stated by the Center for Disease Control.

It was 6:30 AM and I had gone to another persons room to wake him for Mass. After knocking on the other person's door, I heard my name groaned from the other end of the hall. The night lights were still on, so I wasn't sure if there was a light shining under Johnny's door or it was some type of reflection. As I approached,

I could see that it was a reflection on a very dark liquid. I recall being annoyed because I thought he had accidentally spilled soda in his sleep. Opening the door my annoyance turned to horror. Johnny was lying on his stomach with his head over the side of his bed. There was blood all over the 8x12' floor. Putting on rubber gloves and calling to another volunteer, for him to call an ambulance was my immediate action. It was difficult to get Johnny on his back because he complained about pain in his stomach . We were later told that an ulcer in his stomach had ruptured. I assured him that an ambulance was on it's way. I proceeded to clean up the floor and the bed. It is this fact that I often use as proof that the virus can not fly or be contracted by casual contact. If either of these were true, I would be HIV positive. After Mass at 7:45, the Mother Superior appeared at the door of the room, acted shocked and said, "oh, he really does need to go to the hospital. I'll call an ambulance." I was furious and let it be known. This is the problem of bureaucratic obedience at it's worst. The volunteer had told one of the Sisters, who evidently told her superior. She went to Mass first and obviously didn't feel that the volunteers were intelligent enough to know whether or not to call an ambulance. This is one of the reasons I did not join the Missionary of Charity Brotherhood. The Community of St Francis emphasizes individuality and considers the guest's welfare and comfort as paramount. There were many things incorporated in our Community that are a result of negative things that happened at the Catholic Worker and Gift of Peace. Of course, there were tremendous amount of positive circumstances that influence us also. Yeah. I have "screwed up" also.

Gift of Peace is an appropriate name for this exceptional location. It is here that the Lord taught me the true peace that all creatures should have. It is obviously a gradual process. There was an elevation of the persons sent to 2800 Otis Street to a completely different plateau. The Sisters, priests and volunteers, were assured that they were companions in my sojourn and who sought the same goals. The commandment of Christ to "love one another" was personified and made tangible to me. It has since grown to a fullness that is a wonder. I am grateful to all who were involved. Enclosed is another appreciated card produced by the Guests.

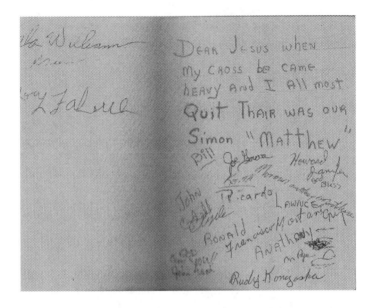

There were many holy and wonderful experiences during my stay. I learned of the diabolic aspects of this dreaded disease. I learn to love those afflicted and deepen my compassion for the person trapped inside that psychological incarceration. The pain isn't all physical and the young have little cognizance of death.

After I left Gift of Peace. I went back to Washington for a number of reasons. I felt that since I was in the area, I would like to visit some of my friends at Gift of Peace. Visiting hours were from 3:00 PM to 5:00 PM.. I rarely went home at that time because of traffic. I went to ask permission to visit in the morning. Having lived and worked there as a volunteer for a year I certainly expected permission to be with people who had in fact been asking about me. I was refused permission and was told I could only come during the visiting hours. I actually did twice but that's not the point. The visiting hours in our Community of St. Francis were from 8:30 in the morning to 9:00 o'clock at night. Of course, there were many positive circumstances that influence us also. Yeah we did well.

"Matt your daughter is on the telephone and would like to speak to you ". Hi dad. I have a question. When are you going to leave Gift of Peace? "I do not know and I have not thought about it. Why do you ask?" We have a problem. Down here in Denton. It involves five teenagers who committed serial suicides. The city government is only addressing the families involved, and nothing else. As you know, because of your dealings with teenagers, there are emotional upheavals at all levels, particularly at a high school level. We have a small group of individuals who understand the problem, but no one is responding to a request. If you can make it down here, get involved, and do your thing it would be a great blessing. I asked "Have you spoken to your pastor? I don't even know his name. I have had only a brief meeting. We shook hands after Sunday Mass". Colleen said "I know his name is Gene Clarahan which is all I know". I don't even know his telephone number. Thirty minutes later I was on the phone with Father Gene. I gave him a brief summary of the psychological effect these horrible things have on the other families and their children. He asked if I could have lunch with him. I could and he was in a small town recuperating from a serious operation The town's name was Cambridge which is something to remember. We went to lunch in the yacht club in Cambridge. I found out that because of his operation he was having trouble running his parish. Does this sound familiar? His secretary was eight months pregnant and would probably not be in the office for a couple of months. Does the term Ministerial Intern, come back into mind. I moved down to his rectory the following Monday. The process of addressing the negative aspects of teenage suicide was started. Eventually we were successful in having conferences with individuals who had been effected and two high school general assemblies. I also spent a portion of my time running the parish with Father Gene's help of course, for about eight months.. We were doing very well at the parish of St. Elizabeth of Hungary a member of the Third Order of St. Francis. My knowledge and background in HIV-AIDS led me to volunteer to help the counties. They were starting to be overwhelmed with the effect of this disease. The effort covered all of the attributes that eventually created the Community of St. Francis.

As usual, there were incidences that required a great deal love and understanding. A friend of mine from church told me about a middle-aged man who wanted to receive Holy Communion. Unfortunately, he felt that the Catholic church has rejected him because he was gay. He attended an Episcopalian Church occasionally, because he was relatively sick with HIV/AIDS. I went and visited him in a town called Bethlehem. We spent a couple of hours together. And I was convinced that there was no reason for him not to receive Communion. "Mark, on behalf of myself and the entire Catholic Church, I ask your forgiveness in the love of the Lord. Forgiveness for all of the pain, distress and desertion that emanated from us to you. Please forgive us and accept my apologies in the love and peace of the Lord." Mark is a wonderfully compassionate individual who spent many of his last days on earth lecturing to groups about the horrors of having

AIDS. His once handsome demeanor was reduced to skin and bone. He was in constant pain and mentally distressed, but never despaired. His message to others was that AIDS could be prevented through common sense. Abstinence from sex or not using needles for drug injection was the only absolutely safe protection. Understanding the nature of the human appetites, he was wise enough to know that many people would not be able to, or want to give up these pleasurable aspects of life. He was frank about his position and honestly answered any question presented to him by members of the audience. Presentations to teens were the most common arena used , and the questions could be brutal. Mark, while often sitting in a wheel chair, would field the questions with a matter of honesty that would thwart any snide or under handed attempt to degrade him or any other person.

Mark loved Jim for more than seven years. Although our friendship was cut short by Mark's death, there were aspects of this relationship that are remarkable. Jim loved Mark as deeply and passionately as Mark loved him. When I met this couple, the outstanding element of their relationship was their compassion and concern for their partner. It was ironic that their intimate life had many aspects of my relationship with my wife. They never parted company without kissing and saying "I Love You". They shared everything. Their daily concerns for planning activities or meals included their partners wants or needs, they held hands, brushed a cheek gently with their fingers and did their best to please their partner.

The most amazing aspect of this relationship was the care for one another when they were sick. Both were diagnosed with AIDS for a number of years. Both had some serious set backs. Jim was the more physically capable of the two, but Mark did what he could to help. The loving, gentle, compassionate attention they practiced was the cohesive element of there relationship. My experience has rarely seen this practice duplicated within a marriage of heterosexual partners. This couple, along with others in a similar relationship negates the contention that gay or lesbian individuals are not capable of having a loving, lifetime commitment before God, to a marital covenant.

He followed the example of millions of Catholics and turned to another congregation where he was accepted as the good person that he was. The Episcopalians accepted him with open arms, even after it became known that he was ill with AIDS. The pastor administered to him regularly, bringing him communion and friendship. Mark confided that, although this was a much needed nurturing, he longed for original communion with Christ and the Roman Catholic Church. After a number of visits, I realized that Mark was an excellent Christian, went to confession and certainly was close to Christ. After explaining to him that Christ comes to us through our Father's love and the vehicle used is unimportant, I fulfilled his wish weekly.

The remembrance of the numerous pictures of persons in concentration camps during WW II emanated on his entire being. Mark was only partially aware that we were in the room. He would reach out his arms as if receiving a loved one. Jim responded with tender embraces, but Mark's yearning seemed to be demanding something else. His eyes seemed focused on something "out there". During our many discussions, Mark became fascinated with the Desert Fathers of the early centuries, particularly the use of "Javelin" prayers. They were short, to the point and hurled at God in rapid succession. We called them aspirations when I was growing up. Mark's personal prayer was "I love you Jesus, thank you for loving me". Remembering this, I whispered it to him. His face was transformed into a ray of light with an enormous smile. This was the last expression he exhibited on this earth. Jim and I remained friends, but were not as close as Mark and I. He continued to live in the same house and had the furniture set up to facilitate one person taking care of himself when he became ill. He had no intention of getting "serious" with any one else. He did not want anyone hovering over him and did a good job of avoiding that. Jim passed on about a year later.

*It should be noted that if one delves into the teaching of the church, they will find that there is a pastoral cloak of love and understanding that falls short only in the sexual marriage of same sex relationships. The premise that sexual intercourse 's main objective is only for procreation has been modified. Taken to the logical conclusion of this modification, sexual intercourse is the fruition of a loving relationship and should not be limited to couples who meet criteria established by humans. Selfish promiscuity, known as pornography, is deviant from the law of nature regardless of the orientation of the participants. This action is true sin.

It is interesting that some none Catholic Bibles describe the Eunuch persons within a nature of homosexuals. (Mt 19 12 : 14). The terms include the fundamentals relating to our current day subject. It makes me wonder.

CHAPTER 2
AGAPE LOVE

"Love is where you find it. Don't be blind. It's all around you everywhere". Those are words from a song back in the 1950s. It was not intentional but they certainly applied to Christ's teaching. He doesn't give us an exact description of what love is or what it means. He does show how it is to effect individuals and what He basically does. He constantly refers to the nonmaterial factors and requires that we take the teaching and put them all together to come up with a life of true love. As I live, study and enjoy this suggested way of life, I can see the presence of this mystical entity. I don't mean physically only or return to it as a spiritual element of our lives. We are so far away from knowing what material existence really amounts to, that it is difficult for people to come to Jesus and comprehend the relationship.

Christ has used the term "Agape" throughout His presentation of the Father's will. It is the ultimate representation of divine love. It basically is the unconditional, self-sacrificing, active, and compassionate relation to an individual. The essential element that Deifies the act is that there is no expected return for the gift. It can only be given away. This tremendously holy action will be referred to frequently in this love story. The term, "agape" is an English translation of an ancient Greek word. It is shown in a variety of Christ's lessons, e.g. the Sermon on the Mount, "love your enemies". We are exposed to after death existence. The presentation involving God the Father indicates that we will lose our physical body. It makes sense . We need eyes to see, ears to hear and a brain to understand. Once we are dead, we no longer need these physical assets. Thus agape love is a universal coagulant that eventually will produce the perfect world. With agape we are filled with Jesus in our body and our soul. The spiritual existence will be the transparent conduit for reaching heaven with God. This is the love connection for which we do not have a distinctive definition. "Agape" is a better suited word, but we tend to just use "love". We need to remember that the word "love" can have a deep spiritual definition that pervades the material as well.

St. Paul does a great job in describing what the absence of love means to existence in his letter to the Corinthian (1 Corinthians 13 01: 13). Using a common everyday type of observance it is easy to see that he's telling people of his era the principle that we are just beginning to learn. This new depth deals with our conception of time. We put it into the projection to the next level of life . We cherish St. Paul's communication and can realize it's importance by the reasoning he uses. It is easy to absorb when he vocalizes his position stating "if I speak the language of men and of angels but do not have love, I am a sounding gong or a clanging cymbal. If I had the gift of prophecy and understand all mysteries and all knowledge. And if I have all faith so that I can move mountains, but do not have love I am nothing. If I donate all my goods to feed the poor, and give my body to be burned But do not have love, I gained nothing. Love is patient: love is kind. Love does not envy, is not boastful: is not conceited; does not act improperly; is not selfish; is not provoked; does not keep a record of wrongs; finds no joy in unrighteousness, but rejoices in the truth; bears all things, believes all things; hopes all things endures all things. Love never ends".

When I was a child (condense a few sentences) For now we see indistinctly as in a mirror but then face to face. Now I know in part, but then I will know fully, as I am fully known. Now these three remain: Faith, Hope and LOVE, but the greatest of these is LOVE.

This is one of the most spiritual individual preacher in our history. What is he trying to tell the people of his time? He covers many of the worldwide episodes to alert the Christians he has educated that there really is only one major factor in our existence. This was about 1,960 years ago, Can you imagine how difficult it was for a slightly educated group to absorb these principles. (I am fairly convinced that this time love was expressed through the Holy Spirit relating back to Christ.)

Paul covers illuminated aspects of dedicating our lives through Christ to love one another. We cannot survive the Cosmic features of the universes until we have combined the ingredients of a million more years on our planet. It is difficult to conjure up the joy, peace, compassion and understanding for all of the elements that are essential for creation. We can only do this through the love of Christ.

We have improved our knowledge of the universes tremendously over the last 2000 years. We have still not come close to understanding what it is and how it completely effects us. We have been told that we are not aware of all of the functional process being used. This shows that we need an education to improve our brain status. This is a mystical impression and influence on the definitions of our existence. The lack of knowledge of these aspects effect our living, language and loving. Pictures of our Universes supports the concept of our lack of knowledge.

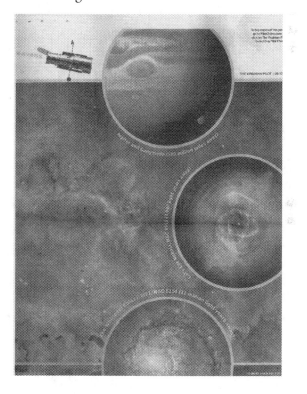

My analysis of the situation shows how deep and fast our creation actually is. Since I am dealing with my own approach, I will describe one analytical attraction. I was always fascinated in some circumstances on Sky Line Drive in Virginia. During a scenic ride, the trees are changing colors at a reasonable, natural rate. An isolated area was made available one day to research . That seems simply natural. The objective was to attempt to count the number of changes that the retina of your eyes will accept, record, analyze and store or reject the data. It became impossible to just collect the initial kind of data. There isn't even a type of mechanism to collect other factors thus it is obviously impossible for us to do the research. We are trying to get a general atmosphere for understanding the depth of the unknown functions of our emotional brain. This gives us a hint as to how much deeper Christ's emotions are and we have to catch up. Lack of understanding love completely is what Christ has recognized in us. Now He is teaching us that eventually we will be over doing 60 miles an hour in the car and accept what is love . This is a phenomenal reaction to our physical bodies that needs knowledgeable acceptance. We are far behind. This is the view of the humble servant as mentioned above.

Another challenge for uncovered earthly functions is the existence of the communication networks. The waves are incomprehensible. We know they are here. We have been able to refine them through sophisticated equipment. Progress over the last 50 years has been accelerated to unbelievable traffic. What are the unique problems? We can not see them without converting equipment. How do the waves penetrate walls or stay with cars at 60 miles per hour? A single word can circulate around the world or into outer space in a NOWment. These things are just like heaven based on Christ's curriculum.

There is a professional mathematical calculation that is called TOE or The Theory of Everything. It was produced by an International Mathematicians Group. It describes the smallest piece of a matter as being a thread like item that is a billion of a trillionth of a trillionth of an inch. WOW, can I see that. Scientists in Europe are producing research on how basically atomic cell construction is. They have discovered an infinitesimal particle that was thought to be the smallest particle of our existence. The item is called the Rigs Particle, after the person who discovered it. It turns out that there was something that left a wake produced by its movement, but the follicle can not be seen, even with a computer. (St. Francis always wanted to be the smallest and most humble person on earth. Maybe that's him) This adds to my philosophy which states that there something a lot smaller than a moment, and it is impossible for us to measure it right NOW. The components and relationships of one person to another in my time is NOW. We know that there are different levels of all that Christ relates to. It is the acceptance that we live in the indescribable incident of no past or no future. Our loving can only be a blessing in the NOW. The NOWment (a Matty Make up word) is the same as the innocence of children. The basic scientific approach or the function of our eyes should be reacting to childlike inhibition when we are loving. This includes the limitations of our emotions. We caught some kind of negative reaction to this invitation. This child's innocence has not gone through life that misdirects themselves or the rest of society. That part of delirium is caused by basically simple, honest loving. Christ presenting an ideal relationship for individuals to obtain (Mt 18-2:5). "Christ was asked by his apostles who will be the greatest in heaven? He called the child to him and assured them that "unless you are converted and become like children you will never enter the kingdom of heaven". Therefore, whoever humbles themselves like this child can become one of the greatest in the kingdom of heaven. Whoever welcomes one child like this in my name welcomes me" That's when the bad influence in our society comes into play and produces a negative metanoia in us . That changes the good person into a not so good person. We allow the decisions to be made based on our experiences that happened today, yesterday etc. We are placed in an unreasonable position. How do we know what the innocents of the child amounts to. Could it mean at the time of birth when the embryo has all of the context that will produce a human being in all of it's beauty. The result will arrive after the elements are processed. That could be the acknowledgement of universal pro-creation. This proves that Christ did not say there is only one way to anoint (baptize) many people. Feeling that you have to be extremely conscious of being sent by Christ in order to be saved was quite the opposite. When you're with Christ, you are sitting there saying "here it is". You will see that happiness comes from being in that loving atmosphere.

Referring to the statement " Here it is", becomes a tremendously challenging observation of what Christ is telling us. He is relating to the future, which we are referring to as heaven. Our limited brain power leaves us gliding in our universe using the map presented by Christ to determine where we should land. The problem surfaces when others make interpretation that isn't the same as the instructions. The reason I keep reverting back to what we consider nature is to put it in perspective. We recognize the existence of material (within our Galaxy) .We are still tremendously ignorant about the objects both outside of our universe and within. If we look at the approach that Christ is using in most of His messages we can see they are contrary or misdirecting to our laws. This will be presented later. This having been said, it looks to me that Christ is showing off. What would be expected outside of our current existence. The reason for this discussion is to point out that there are immeasurable factors in our NOW existence that do not have noticeable effects. However, many individuals require these types of verbal descriptions as their basis for loving Christ or not loving Him. When the Cosmic influence is beyond our capabilities as we look at our desire to identify things such as love, hate, heaven, hell, etc. to the absolute truth. We find that there is still a percentage of our brain being used with knowledge. It is imperative that we absorb the results of these analysis in a spiritual endeavor through Christ's love and absolute knowledge. Leave the creation theory and the others to the limited human factors. Once you accept these results from Christ you become a meaningful servant of the Lord.

A question that has been evoked that can elevate the physical relationship with Christ is "how can we all be one in Him?" There have been a Bazillion residents on earth and He is limited to about 5 ft 2 inches tall and 125 lbs. We accept the fact that nothing can be created or destroyed in our atmosphere. What happened to the elements that constituted His existence when he rose from the dead? Could the perfect loving cellular components be circulating in nature? The objective being that all of us eventually could be completely constructed as one in Christ. All of the cells would be physically related to the Lord. The announcement that Christ made about the second coming could be slightly different. It could relate to His returning thru the method mentioned and He is BEcoming. Not on a cloud but through the actions of our creator. This is an interesting approach. This could also describe purgatory and hell. Floating punishment?

Of course, in the present day it is difficult to accept the negative aspects of Christ's teaching. Just to review the facts when he tells the Apostles that they will be confronted, beaten and possibly killed (as martyrs) just for preaching how to love one another (Mt 24-9:14). This is ludicrous. This also indicates that He is not only of this world. All of our investigation assumes that our life path has to be the same as other existing creatures. We believe that everything must have a beginning and an end. This may not be true. We will find out later. This has to be considered part of our analysis. As we review instances that The Community of Saint Francis (COSF) has bestowed on us, we'll try to indicated how important and meaningful loving approaches have been.

We will review the reaction to the basic teaching at the sermon on the Mount. This is just to point out how one is expected to react to the situation presented by Christ. The Community of Saint Francis tried to react accordingly.

Statement: "as for the one who wants to sue you to take away your shirt, let him have your coat as well."

Reaction: The Community of St. Francis's van was violently crushed in the back by a truck. The accident occurred, because there was a squirrel out in the street, picking up food. (no, he was not making a commercial). The person driving the truck was an employee of the sheriff's office. All other people who were involved, particularly the insurance company representative felt that it was wrong to stop and respect the squirrel. The damage was estimated at $1200. However, the insurance company refused to pay and indicated they were going to court. This would cost us a lawyers fee and use of the van. After analyzing the situation and deciding that Christ would not force someone to do what is right by going to court. I basically conveyed that principle to the deputy. A friend of the community repaired the van for $400. We included the deputy and his family in our evening prayers.

Statement: "You have heard that it was said Love your neighbors and hate your enemy. But I tell you love your enemy, those who persecute you".

Reaction: Our house was sold for not paying back taxes. We are a tax exempt Corporation.

Basically, when we purchased the house, we were supposed to sign a post card claiming to be non taxable. No one told us they kept this operation for four years. There were many address errors in their records. because of this we did not receive any notices. The house was sold without us knowing it We received notice that someone bought it. In order to rectify the action, we had to pay the person who purchased the house all of the expenses he had paid. After we paid him, we were challenged by the city of Cambridge and Dorchester County. We had to pay more money, unfortunately. We went before the councils . Some of the council members spent fifteen or twenty minutes praising us and the work we did. Our efforts were applauded but they refused to rescind the required payment. The most difficult part is to try to understand how this happened. Obviously, there are people who do not want The Community of St. Francis in their neighborhood. Their transaction eventually caused us to close the houses. These our remote enemies who we pray for and show them our love when we can. (Of course , not in our houses).

Statement: "give to the one, who asks you and don't turn away from the one who wants to borrow from You".

Reaction: They are actually three categories we had to accommodate. The third one relates to those who take the money without permission and do not intend repaying. This is the influence of the drug culture. The basic philosophy is, if we have the money and you need it, we will give you the money. There are many instances where we had given to individuals and we required some verification, but in general, they needed the money and would do anything to get it. Walk the street or sell dope etc. On occasion, if I felt that there was a true loving value to help them I would. There are only four individual who actually borrowed money and repaid on a regular basis. Some persons would give us a payment when they receive money from elsewhere. I believe that most of our Guests had the intention of paying us back.

The second category of having someone just needing money that was available to give it, was okay. It helped those living in poverty. It was not an accounting system set up for saving or investing. The first category was out stealing with mechanical transactions. They would steal credit cards, blank checks, Food stamps, independence cards, items to sell and one of our many cars. In most instances I knew what was happening. Confronted the individual and warned them that they could be sent to jail and not be allowed back in the house. On occasion I would dismiss someone from the house, depending on circumstance. Most of the time it just started over again. The person being exposed to the agape often wondered, and generally had a good effect. I did not send anyone to jail in the 18 years I've been in Cambridge. The money exchange was within hundreds of thousands of dollars.

Another level of charity is where a member of the Intentional Community performed some managerial functions for us. These were directing conferences, attending meetings and public relations. He was unemployed and had need for financial assistance .We provided a great deal of money with no objection. Around 1997 I had just counted a pile of cash twice. I was going to the bank. This gentleman was in the office. As soon as I finished counting, a guy came in with a wound and had to go to the hospital. I put the money in the petty cash box and put it in the desk draw. Something told me to put a ribbon over it for security sake. The trip to the hospital took 15 minutes. When I came back to the office and took out the box the ribbon had been moved. I recounted the money. Forty dollars were missing. I told him and suggested he just return it and all will be forgiven. He claimed he left the office and someone must have entered the house and took it. I told him that was not true and I am accusing you of stealing. He emptied his pockets and of course the money was not there. I just made the statement that $40.00 could buy an "8 ball" right out back. He left being aware that I felt he had stolen the money. Our friendship remained but for years the same type of incident occurred. One time he declared he gave a Mexican family $100.00. However, he didn't get any personal information from them. These are being splashed out because the love stream was still flowing. Practically every month he needed help. My decisions were effected by the presence of his wife. She is exceptionally blessed. They both are religious and active in their church. My intention is to provide them with exposure to what God is expecting. Hopefully it will be adopted. This is a complete application of the "agape principle."

The turning of other cheek was not as prevalent. We had three gentlemen who weighed around 250 - 300 pounds and were 6 foot.4 inches plus. Generally if the situation arose that would be potentially violent, these gentlemen were there to support me. On other occasions, my Jersey City personality would show up and handle most other circumstances.

One of the reasons was an exaggeration rumor that stemmed from a minor incident. It was late at night and I was helping one of my protectors move into his new apartment. The van was parked under a street light. This created an area that was super dark. As I walked toward the back a huge body jumped out of the shadow and shouted BOOO. Before he regained his balance, I punched him twice in the stomach and came within inches of his jaw. The reaction was primarily due to daily Ti Chi. I assure you if it was serious as soon as the third punch landed I would have hauled ass. (Jersey language). The story was told at the house and then forgotten. Over the next couple of months the depicture of the results grew to me beating him up and knocking him out. He accepted the phony part to allow the incident to force aggressive individuals to think twice before attacking me. This was an Agape extension. I was never attacked physically. There were times when I attempted to prevent violence and had to use psychiatric specialist training to reduce potential injury.

These are instances, just to show how we had the Community conveying the love of Christ by performing according to His teaching. There are many other instances that we perform in the agape mode that is not approved by fellow servants.

Many of my brothers and sisters who have devoted their lives to Christ had the opinion that Christ specifically said you had to go through him, physically, to get to heaven or "to be saved ". I go again to the principle and see how these teachings are related to the loving outcries. A number of times in the Bible Christ refers to it being involved as a part of each individual on earth. Since he made it clear that each person has Christ living in them it means he is part of them. Mother Teresa of Calcutta often expresses her love for the Christ who was present in the person in front of her. This ensures the proper relationship with everyone throughout the day. Taking this posture would be dealing with hundreds, even thousands of individuals who are "in front of us.". You can now extrapolate the principle that if Christ is a truthful person when we do a loving and compassionate act we are performing them directly through Him. Remember Christ reminded us that He was in the Father, and the Father was in Him and He was in us.(John 17, 21:23) This is the prayer to the Father .Therefore what we are doing with individuals (regardless of how difficult it is to recognize Christ in their " distressing disguise". That is a Mother Teresa Quote. Many people can see how by loving someone who has Christ in them they are directly dealing with Christ. You are still going to heaven, through Christ who is currently included in your life. It is easy to show loving and compassionate care for people who are well. It is much more difficult to serve Guests who are not obviously acting Christ-like. They could easily be performing negative activities that are against God's law. Personal decisions are the aspect of understanding both sides of the teaching that comes directly through the gospel. There is always some good factor within any individual. The exercise of religion, of it's very nature consists for all else. This involves, voluntary and free acts whereby anyone sets the course of his life directly toward God, negative or positive. No merely human power can either command or prohibit acts related to God.

The parable of the good Samaritan, presented the three individuals who ignored the person who had been beaten up. If we go, and research what each of those three people were we will find out that they were obeying the law of Moses and Abraham. The following tradition, not to work on the Sabbath, not to touch bleeding persons and not to perform religious rituals outside of the temple were acceptable rules in the Jewish religion. These men were not bad men. They followed the rules. Whereas the Samaritan, a strong enemy of the Israelites in Jerusalem was in a perfect position to also say no to helping. This loving Jew followed his heart and not only help the individual but took care of him later. The major principle in this parable is to help your neighbor through love according to your conscience. There is this type of love in your heart to the Lord, when it is given away with no strings attached. This is "Agape" there should be nothing expected to return. It is difficult for us to accept the fact that no matter how wonderful our actions are many times they are not accepted. There are many persons and groups who will not even recognize the good in what we do. Your reaction through this parable should give you an idea of what Christ was telling us. The basic transaction was good, compassionate and wonderfully beneficial to the victim. He does not condemn the other people who did not act according to his teachings . Did he put the good Samaritan on a pedestal?

You can see that the teachings that come from the parables, the miracles, and the general everyday conversation revolve around enabling. Studying basic principles will assure everyone who can understand the value of love for one another will be able to have a happy life. When you get into some of the things that are really difficult it could take a life time. It can demand a lot of effort to meditate on what is being said and apply it to your own life. Some things are not acceptable in the world. We discuss from both viewpoints that which Christ has told us and that which nature of all different types of religion tell us also. Basically we have problems with the quotes "love your neighbor as yourself,. forgive 70 times seven , turn the other cheek, give your cloak, don't stone women for committing adultery". These are only a few of the actions that are addressed by Christ. They illuminate the aspects of dedicating our lives through Christ to love one another.

THE ENABLER

"You are a menace to our society by allowing these people to survive to commit more crimes". "You are jeopardizing your neighbors physical safety and their valuable possessions!" "You are enabling individuals who are living on the wrong side of our law to continue to break the law". "This is contrary to our beliefs and our rights". "You should be put in jail also".

These types of comments are often directed at the Community of St. Francis. Comments relate to a variety of different neighborhood concern, such as the value of my home being reduced. The people who visit you are terribly vulgar, filthily dressed, aggressive, despicable in nature. When the subject is approached by professional psychologists they will tell you that an individual who may be an addict, criminal or mentally challenged should receive special service. Usually it is a process to separate them from our society. There are some individuals who indeed have to be incarcerated to protect themselves and others from potential violence. This leaves a group of people who are basically unemployed, homeless and with some sort of addiction and on their own to face a very difficult life. Because of this approach, we only put them further away from the One who is teaching us how to show our loving, understanding and compassionate lifestyle. Over the last 20 years I have heard this type of criticism time and time again in both medical and social gatherings. Understanding the true implication of loving one another and being a Franciscan is awesome. We share everything we do basically with the principle of God's love as the incentive for all action. My concern is that almost everyone wants to condemn our approach to enabling an individual. They will not stop and think for a minute, whether or not, there is another direction for the enabling act. We are expected to accept the single ,non-dynamic, violations. These punishments relate to various acts that are contrary to our pursuit of living.

Let us see if we should now analyze the enlightened part of enabling.

First, let's define "enabling" To provide someone with the authority, resource or opportunity to do something. (Note that there is no mention of being bad or good).

Unfortunately most people do not indulge it in a positive atmosphere. It is generally related as an action that is negative. You rarely hear that a priest or a nun is enabled to complete their vocation. Sooo, who do you think is the most well known "enabler" on this earth? How does His approach relate to our daily life? Is it Christ? Let's go to the Bible again and find what it is and do we acknowledged it. ((MT, 18, 21:35) The kingdom of heaven can be compared to a king who deals with an unforgiving servant. -------

So my heavenly father will also do to you, if each of you do not forgive his Brother from his heart"

We will begin with one statement that we are instructed to follow. If you can apply in the total philosophy after 2000 years you will be enlightened and loving. As we mentioned before, Peter asked Christ how often should I forgive my brother? Seven times? Christ responded "no, it should be seventy times seven". The point He was making was not numeric. (we are not obliged to carry a calculator to determine results). If one does not forgive the individual for their breach of the law or the infringements on some ones rights, we are back to 32 AD. What He is basically saying is that if you in fact do not allow your loving posture, energized by the Holy Spirit, to accept the individual back into your life, (with some adjustments, if necessary) infinite forgiveness cannot be applied. An individual who has returned to your neighborhood after they have been out in society is potentially a saint. You must accept the people who come to you one person at a time as a distressingly disguised Christ in front of you. You have to forgive the individual, the action required and let them come back time and time again. You enhance your position as a compassionate loving servant of God and react positively again and again and again. This is not an easy thing to do. Many people will not even listen when we are merely following Christ's teaching .

Here is an example about four similar incidences that subjectively, give us a different view on different levels of understanding and reaction. If someone has committed a crime that requires them to be sent to jail it can drop them out of our community. This of course is not true. As a Franciscan, we will still go and visit them and/or write them letters. When they get out of jail ,we will go to pick them up and give them shelter. They are now back in line for potentially being enlightened. This also indicates that one cannot be found if they are not lost. These situations have happened frequently and provides a great reward for our efforts. There is also a requirement of the defining what constitutes the various levels of success.

A different type of enabling circumstance could go into court because you trusted a person to obey the functional rules of the House. The rules were reviewed when a person arrives. These incidences revolve around long-distance telephone calls that were not performed with criminal intent. The house rules for an individual specifically stated that you are not to make long distance telephone calls at all. Assuming everyone will follow the rules, we did not receive the large telephone bills for at least one and a half months. As was mentioned before four guests utilized the telephone for more than $5,000 worth of calls. Each person is different and they ran up the bills for different reasons. The expected response to this type of thing would be to throw them out of the house. Of course, they could also be required to pay it back or go to jail. We also had to use a different telephone system for months. Our dark side assumes we are doing right. When in fact, Christ is telling the whole world "it is not so" . You should want to love the poor and support them on every level. These subjects we are visiting are enabling action of a positive nature. If one takes a look at the many sessions in the Bible they will find that Christ is enabling each person individually via the response to produce a positive loving service.

Evaluating the results of our approach, must also be done on a positive concern with the effect. Having followed my understanding of Christ's love, I have succeeded. Exploding all positive emotions into an individual's persona ensures happiness and functional spirituality in our society. There are other incidences that do not necessarily fit into my definition of a related path. For instance, there were four couples who were introduced to each other at the Community of St. Francis. and got married.

The references above were included to show the variety of activities that occurred at the Community Hospitality House. There were many more incidences with the same type action but with a different cast. However there is one character who fulfilled almost all aspects of portraying the issuance of our Agape Love. We will discus him later.

Chapter 3
HOME SWEET HOME

The voice on the other end of the phone said, "I have a woman who has a house for you." It had been almost a year since I left the Missionaries of Charities. I am living in Ridgely MD with Fr Gene Clarahan. I have been doing volunteer work for the Dorchester County Social Services. My main area was persons with the HIV/AIDS virus. The voice on the phone was the social worker who was responsible for AIDS patients on the Eastern Shore. She was one young lady who was blessed and worked hard to bring comfort and help to persons who were afflicted with AIDS. Her name is Pat Finley. She deserves as many accolades as I could dream of and twice as many thanks.

An example of what is meant by simply living the Gospel and the current trends would be illustrated by an actual conversation at an introductory meeting of the Caroline County Health Dept. AIDS Task Force on the Eastern Shore of Maryland. "Matt, what organization do you belong to?" "The Secular Franciscan Order." "To

Whom do you report?" "No one." "Then who is your boss?" "God" "How did I know you were going to say that. You have to understand that we have never met anyone like you before." At first it was amusing, then it became a sad commentary on our supposed Christian society. Make no mistake there are many, people who do similar types of things that the author does, but our current society is reluctant to meet them.

We agreed that there was a need for a home for individuals who are sick with HIV/AIDS and homeless. I had been looking for a house in the Ridgely/Denton area for some time, but my efforts were fruitless. Then, Thump! from the left field.. Are you starting to wonder, who is playing left field? There is a house in Cambridge, MD. Ironically, it was in Cambridge where I had lunch with Fr Gene and he graciously allowed me to move into the rectory at St Benedict's.

We met the woman the next morning and agreed to look at the house. I honestly expected a shanty or handyman's special in the "wrong side of town". I was pleasantly surprised. The house was old, but had a beautiful kitchen, 3 bedrooms, dining room and was partially furnished. It was a well kept neighborhood, only half a block from the Choptank River. Our neighbors were mostly elderly women who did not need any added worry for their safety. We decided that we would limit our clientele to individuals who were at the later stages of AIDS and not likely to be roaming the neighborhood. "And all will be well" as Julian of Norwich would say.

I had saved money through donations to the Community and was very cost conscious. As Division Director for the U. S. Postal Service I was responsible for closing the books. So if this woman thinks she has a "patsy" she is sorely mistaken. I cannot afford more than five hundred dollars a month, including utilities. I really liked the house, but kept reminding myself to stick to my guns. I noticed that there were no Religious articles.

We were in this beautiful kitchen and the folding door to the pantry was broken. Joan, the landlord, said, "let's go into the living room and discuss the rent. I'll want six hundred dollars per month. This will include utilities." Ding, ding, ding, oh no it won't . Five hundred, that's it. Period. I'm a strong business man and cannot afford to let anything sway me. WRONG! As we are about to leave the kitchen, Joan says, "oh, let me close that door." She goes back to the broken folding door and closes it. On the wall behind the door is the cross of San Damiano. Give me a break! It means nothing .How come there weren't any other religious articles in the house? No, I am not changing. A thought came into my head, Wasn't this the cross that gave Francis his most important message? No, this is to be my house. No, well maybe have you anything better? but for six hundred dollars? O.k., o.k., I hear you. We went inside and I agreed to the six hundred with utilities. It later changed to $500 and we paid the utilities. Afterward, I asked Joan if she knew what that cross was and she said, "no". I asked if she knew how it got there? She said, "no". WOW! It certainly was a sign and was effective. The message was clear and the Lord saw to it that the cross would be seen. An interesting side light to that bit is that I left the cross on that wall all of the time we lived there. Just before moving to Church Creek, M.D. Joan had a new back door put in which eliminated that wall. I have no idea where the cross is. You have to wonder.

This is the first episode of a remote individual having an effect on our operation. A year after moving into the first house I was told that a woman, who worked at the Dorchester County Mental hospital had informed Pat that the building was available. The lady's name is Bonnie Barnidge aand she is a tremendous help. I've finally got to meet her. It turned out that she was also a member of the Presbyterian Third Order of St. Francis. This was the beginning of the influence of persons who are operating at an unknown relationship. We became good friends, and she helped establish a fraternity for the community. The group was ecumenical in nature and we met at her home. It is amazing how the Lord can be effective without immediate interface.

The house on Choptank Ave. turned out to be the most defining element of my being in the house of the Lord. I had never realized the significance of living with the marginalized members of our society. The major factor was not being away from family and friends. It was being with persons who are in no way similar to you in culture, belief or life style. During the year that I lived with the Missionaries of Charity, there were some elements of this. We lived in the same building, but our rooms were in a separate section. There were others performing the same type of actions. Philosophically I was alone. Much too liberal and almost heretical to the sisters. I often felt I was doing my "Desert Time". Even now, after twenty years of working with thousands of citizens.

You might feel that this is extreme, but it is true. At Choptank Ave. there were a few persons who came to help me. Unfortunately they were committed elsewhere or in need themselves. The most outstanding, humble Franciscan Brother, Vianni Justiin was the best teacher/servant that God sent to assure my success. He would come down to Choptank Ave. and run the house for the weekend while I could have a break. He is an exceptional Franciscan.

I do distinguish between the segments of the Community of St Francis. There are those in the Community in need of our attention (the community of attention). The volunteers constituted the Community of intention (willingly living in a communal arrangement at COSF). The extended community consists of those who support us with prayers and financial assistance. So far, the desert dweller is the only person in the community of intention. This was, and is, glaring by appearance but as Julian of Norwich would say "all will be well". There are times that I wonder where the "others" are, but I am constantly learning that we live in the Lord's time (or existence) not ours. I feel I built it as in The Field of Dreams. Now. it is up to them "to come". It is important to understand that solitude in the midst of our crowded world is a pleasant state. I am not complaining, just verifying

When we agreed to rent the house, within two hours all three beds had been assigned to individuals. The first was a woman who was in her early eighties and had the qualifications needed to live with us. She was a very classy dresser with a summer umbrella and always looked nice. The second sentence after I met her included 1. I am a tough cookie. 2. I will have a lot of visitors. 3. You do not know how to cook Greens. She taught me how before she left.

Ron arrived at the Community of St. Francis on February 28, 1991. He was the numero uno member of the Community. He didn't know how to be mean or aggressive, although other Guests were very difficult to get along with. High school teenagers and other group invited COSF to give presentation relating to AIDS. Ron was very happy to be part of it. This is where the change of approach and vocalizing tone on his every word, were very good, They had to pay attention because it came out very slowly and sometimes incorrect. The theme was always radiant and the audience loved him. After he had passed on we still received cards and letters from individuals and groups.

Cherubic was the only way to describe the face of this beautiful man. His face splitting grin could light up an entire room. He was 28 years old but can easily pass for 15 years old.

The slow speech and difficult comprehension problems were manifestations of the HIV / AIDS virus. It was screwing up the nerve network in his brain. He would have very extreme convulsions and or short-term memory loss,

Shortly after he arrived, I was in the kitchen and I heard a blood curdling scream. I went running through the house to locate the source. This was a warm day, which meant that many windows were open in the house. Finding out where it was coming from was difficult. Since it was not in the house. I went out the front door. The origin of the siren like scream was Ron just two steps off the porch. He had gone out the door, down two steps, and mentally became terrifyingly lost. Bounding out of the house. I immediately looked for some injury, blood or some attacking animal. As soon as I embraced him he squatted down and sobbed volcanically. This type of thing happens often, but without the physical routine.

One night I was sitting on my bed, reading my prayer book (my daily office). Ron came to the door and asked if we could pray together. Of course! Come on in and sit down. I began to read the Psalms out loud. He was very solemn and attentive. We said the Our Father, a few other prayers and we were finished. We sat there for some quiet meditation minutes. I thought it was real nice that he was reflecting on our praying when he said, "Can we pray for real now?" I told him that I did not understand what he was saying. His explanation simple. We are going to kneel down, close our eyes and shout AMEN every now and then. We followed his instructions but limited the amount of the Amens.

In another incident that highlighted his problem, one night we were having sliced roasted beef with gravy over toast with a vegetable. When I announced the menu Ron said "I don't want any meat". That's okay with me. So I just gave him bread and gravy. He came in, sat down and went into a tirade screaming ". I told you I didn't want meat." He became more irate and screamed louder, got up from the table and stomped out of the kitchen. I went after him, calmed him down and asked him to show me what was wrong. We went back into the kitchen, and he went to his plate and pointed to the bread and said. "See, you gave me meat". I took away his plate and scrounge up some meat for him. We then agreed that he would point to what ever we were talking about to be sure we would both be on the same page.

This was just another unstable version of his mental problems. Ron went to Johns-Hopkins Hospital, where special diagnoses and treatment were rendered. They prescribed a new drug called Alpha Interferon. It did wonders for him. His memory improved drastically and speech was almost normal. He could go for short walks by himself. This improvement also allowed him to visit with his family overnight. Of course he was ecstatic.

The one negative thing that most people with AIDS, had difficulty understanding is the diabolical nature of the unpredictable onslaught of a variety of illnesses. The patient becomes ill, is treated with medicine and feels good. Then out of nowhere comes another disease and the roller coaster effect starts all over again. It is difficult to the remain compassionate and loving when you know the relentless wrath of the devastating, incurable invasion.

Ron improved over a couple of months. Then the old symptoms returned twice as strong. He was very depressed because he had tremendous pain that seemed to be appendicitis, along with all the other infections. His mental posture, deteriorated to the point that it had to be supervised. 24 hours. The doctors told him he needed an operation, but there was only a 30% chance that it would be successful. Due to the problems with other symptoms and the AIDS infection, he gave his approval. He was admitted to the hospital but before they operated, his stomach started to swell. I went to visit him and he was completely irrational. I had to physically hold him down in the bed. His actions were jeopardizing all of the medical equipment that he was attached to. I had to leave. So I warned the nurse about the problem and left. When I got home, there was a message from the hospital that he had gone to the Lord.

There was an argument with his family when I asked if I could mention that he had AIDS. His father and grandmother had no objection they knew that Ron was a strong advocate for educating the public about AIDS. The rest of the family were firmly against it, but finally the pastor of the church convinced the rest of the family that it was proper to do so.

Everything I have included in this brief vignette shows the microcosm of what is to be expected in all kinds of circumstances. It reflects many of the situations that we had to approach over the 18 years. The events described here will be present in almost all of the persons in our program. Over the years, it is important that we relate to the events that are the teachings of Christ and the humble servants at the Community of St. Francis. It will all be encompassed in the love of Christ. "All will be well" As Julia of Norwich reminds us again.

Four months later, another young gentleman came to live at the house. His name was Scott and he was the typical individual that we would have to deal with. He had the AIDS affliction but he physically looked healthy. The characteristic I'm referring to is a conniving nature that he used every day. The most common action he would take was to set up a new person to violate the rules and then "squeal" to me and get them in trouble. He was also a drug addict, which usually automatically makes him a professional thief. This was the beginning of my belief of Christ's message forgive many times over. I am of the opinion that it's certainly worth it even though others refuse to accept the principle at the second or third time something went stolen. It was a challenge, and he stayed with us for nearly a year. He was a major personality in our loving orchestra. He was involved in an interesting set of events noted later on.

The community worked well and accomplished their mission. Needless to say, the AIDS epidemic is getting worse, and we opened a second house and this house was in Church Creek, MD. There was a specific criteria. Should you became too sick to take care of yourself in the first house. We would move you to the new house, which was a ranch style. This was also beneficial for me even though I was in excellent shape. The rooms were smaller but overall were much better for those who were bed ridden. The guests help out in the original house so I could operate pretty much on my own. There were a number of interesting characters at church Creek. Each one was unique, and I enjoyed their company.

The operation conducted at Church Creek was unique and highly rewarding. Each person who arrived had a limitation to their presence. Most of them could not even get out of bed. There were unheard of diseases that were difficult to apprehend.

This is the best example of how we were the positive enablers for more than an 18 year period. It started out as a desperate health circumstance, and through the existence of the Community of St. Francis it has been the dwelling place for unusual individuals. Such as a gentleman who had a hole in his colon ,who needed his diaper changed 21 times in a 24 hour period. That particular person seemed pretty healthy when he told me ,around 10 o'clock at night, that he was going to die before the morning. Surprisingly, his prediction was true. When I was in his room at seven o'clock in the morning. He was dead. His physical problems, the hole in his colon was not the cause of his death. The doctors could not declare the reason, because there did not seem to have a legitimate cause. Other instances one young lady asked everyday to please put a pillow over her head and let her be out of this world. Of course, she wanted me to hold the pillow tight. I explained to her that that was not within my philosophy, but I would use pain management to help her make the trip the way God wants it. Another woman had multiple diseases, but all she wanted was a shot of whiskey. She also had an ulcer in her stomach. and it would be a disaster to give her whiskey. She said she was willing to pay me $100 for the drink. I explained to her that the pain would be unbearable and I could not do that. The next time I gave her medicine for pain I liquefied it and gave it to her in and shot glass. She appreciated it, then told me that she really didn't have one hundred dollars. I simply said, in that case, lets pray together for a quick reunion with our Creator. She died the following week.. These are just reflections on how the love of God and the poor serving individuals act on any given day. There are other situations that are the exact opposite type of Christ's direction.

Those were unusual individuals. We had other relationships with everyday life. Gary, the first person, became very good friends with me and my family. Early in June of 1994, I received a phone call from three friends who were associated with the Eastern Shore Psychiatric Hospital. Each wanted to tell me about this great guy who was a patient there. He was HIV positive but asymptomatic and would be terrific as a guest at our house. We had been going through a series of difficult quests so the vision of having a pleasant guest was energizing. Of course, none of these friends were empowered to have presented a verbal resume that piqued my curiosity. I asked the Department of Social Services to look into the possibility of having him at the House and "Voila" Gary was here.

There is not a single complaint I can dream up about him. He was cheerful, witty, quick on the repartee and gave me no quarrels. His politeness was extra ordinary and he never complained. It was a pleasure to have him around. He had done a few too many "wise cracks" and might have a memory lapse, but that was it. He called the seizure his "station" times. Being Catholic, I thought he was referring to the Stations of the Cross and was pleased, "NOTT!" The reference was to a train station.· Once the train is gone all you can do is stand there and wait for it to come back. That explained why he would occasionally go into a trance and stare at the wall. I 'd ask if he was all right and he would say, "nope, the train still out."

Gary endeared himself to my family as it was common for him to come with me (and Buck, the dog) when we went visiting. We would walk into my daughter's house and there would be a chorus of shouts, "hide the food, Gary's here." Believe me, the man was a major with a knife and fork. He could eat! His portion was usually double of anyone else, particularly if we were at a restaurant. We went food shopping together each week. Once, knowing his appetite, I suggested that he go and pick out whatever cookies he wanted for the week. He came back with a large bag of generic animal crackers. That's all he wanted. When we got home I tasted them and they tasted like saw dust. Pointing out the fact that he could have gotten any cookies he wanted, I asked why he picked those. He said, "no one has ever let me do that, so I thought I'd start cheap and work my way up to the "chips Ahoy".

Gary talked to the screen at the movies. It was a little embarrassing but often humorous. We went to see a picture that was full of violence, "The Getaway". Early in the movie the "good guy" has a gun point at the "bad guy" and Gary yells "shoot him, shoot him". Cringing, I tried to be as invisible as possible. The movie goes on and you guessed it, the "bad guy" now has a gun pointed at the "good guy". Loudly, and with disgust, Gary says, "see,

I told you to shoot him before." After a few months, we were joined by a New York Puerto Rican who also yelled at the screen. Fortunately, there were five theaters, so we (me and the others) could go elsewhere or sit as far away from these "public disturbers" as possible.

We had a particularly demanding patient who would call for me as soon as I would step foot in the door. (remember Scott) Gary took great delight in singing the lines from Nelson Eddies hit with a few changes. "He'll be calling you ,ou ou ou ou ou. He hasn't got a clue uue ue ue ue. He has something for you to do 0 0 0 0 o. If you don't he'll cry boo hoo hoo. That was Gary.

His medical care was provided by the V.A. since he was a veteran. He became ill and was admitted to the VA Hospital at Perry Point, MD. It is about a three hour drive so his family and our group tried to get up to see him on a interim schedule. He was there for a number of months. The first time we went to see him, he was shackled to the bed, in a stupor. The shackles were necessary because he kept pulling out his I.V. connection. His medicine was not very powerful so I inquired why did he seemed so unresponsive. The nurse mentioned that he responded to verbal stimulation but that was all. I asked where were his glasses? Her response was, "he wears glasses?" They were in the night table drawer. Once they were on, his eyes lit up and he said "shit, the train's back." There seemed to be no reason why he couldn't come home since we are capable of administering all of the medicine and nutrition, through a tube in his nose. The doctors agreed. At home I started to feed him through the tube and we had an awful time. Our doctor suggested that I take the tube out and see what happened. I did. Gary lit up like a Christmas tree and said he wanted two Big Mac's. I let him know that the likely hood of him being able to keep anything solid down was minimal, but I'd get it for him. As I was going out the door he yelled, "and a large French Fries". It was only a couple of bucks, so I humored him and got everything he asked for. The next three hours I spent with a pot at the side of his bed and asking every fifteen minutes, "are you O.k.?" He finally asked me to sit down next to him and in a very quite, serious tone he said, "I'll have eggs, bacon and waffles for breakfast with coffee." The man could eat!

Gary was my hero in as much as he accepted all faiths. He told me he was Catholic, so we went to mass together. I noticed that he did some non-cradle Catholic things like genuflect on the wrong knee and didn't kneel at the right time, but this was the new way, so I let it go. He received Communion properly with the reverence expected and all was well. About a year later, he told me he was Catholic, but only for a short time. He tried all different religions. The most important being is "the one I'm in now". All of these good qualities could be traced to his parents. His family supported him throughout his illness. His mother is a wonderful person and his father equally so in a different manner. They are the only family that has contacted me after the death of their loved one. It's been years since Gary passed on to his reward, but I still get an occasional call just to see how I am. They also gave me a donation "for me

The ministers and priests allowed me to be with many persons who have died. There is always a grieving period and a loss, but in most instances, the period is brief. When asked how do I survive, I answer, "I don't know.

The analogy of a Thanksgiving dinner usually helps. The guest is invited to the feast, we share the banquet, it ends, I clean up the dishes and go to the next feast. The cleaning up involved notifying the doctor, the family and cleaning the body for the undertaker. In Gary's case, the dishes never really got put away. He is one of the few friends that I met on the journey, who is still present spiritually and still brings an occasional smile to my life.

As the prison guard hefted three large boxes from the back of the cage lined correctional institution van, I was dumbfounded. I was to pick up a man, 26 years old, from prison. What were in these boxes? "clothes and shit", replied the officer. He then went to the side door, opened it, and invited the person to step out. There was John in all his glory, looking like a nineteen year old "rapper". There were no immediate signs of illness, but a smile that crescents his face. At this time it was not the bright, delightful smile I learned to enjoy later on in our relationship. It was disarming. We had not met before, which was unusual, so he was cautious.

I piled the huge boxes into the hatchback of my Sundance with much grunting and groaning, and we were on our way. John was quiet mannered and only spoke as a response to questions. He was scheduled to go to the community house for ambulatory guests. The flight of stairs up to his bedroom afforded me some more grunting time, but that was what I was there for. As I descended the stairs, after the third box, John informed me that he is going home to Easton, MD, which is about 15 miles north of where we were in Cambridge, MD. I simply replied, "I don't think so." He huffed up his chest, put his finger on my chest and presented as tough an attitude as he could and hissed through his teeth. "Listen, Motha Fucka, I said I am going to Easton." I was counting to ten real fast and there must have been fire in my eyes because when I looked down at his finger in my chest, he recoiled it and said he didn't mean to touch me. I hissed through my teeth that I did not want any violent incidents because the neighbors were not crazy about us being here in the first place. He called me a MF one more time as he was walking to the door of the house. All was well.

He was prison laden, did not like other people to be around him and was extremely quite. He showed a great deal of respect to me, but once I set a foot out the door for any extended period of time, he was a terror.

As the months went by, he got thinner and had to be hospitalized twice. Ho joy, he was asked to go to our second house in Church Creek, MD (close to, but smaller then Cambridge) which was dedicated to persons in the later stages of AIDS. Of course, this is where I lived, and I was ecstatic. He adjusted well but spent much of his time in his own room watching TV. He often talked about wanting to go out and have some fun.

Translation - smoke dope and have a woman. John was not Don Juan and lacked the social graces that were usually learned as one leaves puberty. Of course, six years in prison will have some retardant effect. This desire for "fun" would eventually lead to him being thrown out of the house for bringing drugs into the house. Yes, we took him back,

The fact that he thought that I could send him back to prison with the snap of my fingers boggled my mind. Whenever the opportunity presented itself, he opted to do the wrong thing. I could not understand how he could disregard potentially going back to prison. He had eight more years to complete his sentence. later, as we became good friends, he told me that he did take one day at a time, but today had nothing to do with tomorrow. "If today I'm free and have fun, I'm going to have fun. If tomorrow I'm in jail, hell, I've been there before." I guess that's a watered down version of "One day at a time".

The whole philosophy is to beat "the Man" regardless of who he is. He didn't have a major drug problem but he just wanted to break the rules. He told me the marijuana didn't do anything for him. Duh! Maybe it was because he was getting the same thing daily in pills. John went to his aunt's house for Thanksgiving. He was in a wheel chair and had difficulty controlling his hands. I picked him up on Friday and took him home. As we got in the house and he announced he had to pee real bad, I ran in, got a urinal, he stood up in his sweat suit and I just pulled down his pants. As he finished the "ahhh" of relief, it was followed by "Ah Shit". Following his line of sight I saw a bag of marijuana and cigarette rolling paper. When I suggested that he was "dissing" me. He just said, I had nothing to do with it. He never thought about the potential of burning down the house or dying in a flaming bed.

John had an enduring smile that became more pronounced as he became thinner. The last couple of months we became close. We prayed together and talked about love. love of God, one another and his family. During the next to last visit with his mother, he was able to use the word, with difficulty, but fondly. "I love you Ma", he said, then I told him to open the car window and repeat it so she could hear. The attached note shows us his thoughts and how he expresses it.

These are the moments that make all the trying times worthwhile. It is difficult to tell a person they have to leave the house for any reason. When it is in direct violation of the rules that are well known, it is also disappointing. John was thrown out and put into a motel. Total darkness except for the TV, snacks his primary food and few visitors all added to my consternation. We were going to Ocean City, MD for an afternoon so we decided to invite him. He didn't want to go! Eventually, he did join us. We came home, had pizza and John threw up twice. It did not bother him that he threw up in the restaurant, or the doorway, he specifically said, "The owner can clean it up". No concern for the sight, the potential for spreading germs or the fact that the personnel at the restaurant knew he had AIDS. This, again, shows a marked difference in our. prospective. John had the right ideas, but they just didn't surface at the right time. He was rarely nasty, usually polite and had a good sense of humor. Included at the end of this chapter there is an essay I found in his belongings after he died. It is proof that in 1992, he had a good grasp of the theology of the marginalized. All of his swagger and attitude was necessary and very real to him. So was God. He never complained about pain because he was tough. He never pronounced the word "love" because he was tough. He "was gonna make 1996 and did not fear death because he was tough. At the end of his life here on earth, 7:32 am on January 2, 1996, he left at peace with himself in love from God through us. He was tough in accepting his death , but knew the gentleness of the pain free journey. I can only aspire to being as tough and accepting as my good friend John.

I AM

Bolting awake in my bed, I quickly look at the clock and see that it is 5:47 a.m. Through the crust of sleep I try to discern what it was that woke me up. As I was muddling through the haze a loud noise, a pounding crunched the door and a voice yelled, "I want my coffee", another pounding and another demand. My Franciscan demeanor was trampled by a rage. I got out of bed and went into the room next to mine. I held my temper and told him it wasn't even six o'clock yet and he would have to wait until eight o'clock which was the normal breakfast time. He said it was not that early, although he was capable of seeing the clock that was beside his head. All of the frustration of months of humble servitude related to obvious malicious behavior and multiple weeks of sleep deprivation exploded forth. I grabbed his pillow and forcibly moved his head around so he could see the clock and screamed, "why would I lie about a thing like that?" I realized that this was a dangerously aggressive state of mind that could easily result in my hurting this person. I wanted to punch him!

At 8:00 a.m. I called Social Services, explained the circumstances and asked them to get him out of our house for his own safety. They did so, that morning. This was a man who was dying of AIDS.

I was devastated. How could I have let myself lose control? How un-Franciscan can you get? Guilt was rampant. This man had lived with me for 2 1/2 years. He felt we were very close friends and called me Dad. When the people came to bring him over to the hospital he was crying profusely and screaming. "daddy, don't let them take me, please, please" . I told him I was sorry but I felt it was the right thing to do. He immediately stopped crying, sat up on the gurney, pointed to a pillow and said "That's my fucking pillow and they are my cigarettes. He then turned his back and they left. It is, and always has been, my goal to bring peace to those at the house and help them be at peace with themselves. This guy fought it all the way, but I still tried. He came to us as a street person with a penchant for causing friction. The biggest disappointment I have had in the ministry was that this man left our house exactly the same person he was when he came to live with us. In my opinion, he was the only person who did not die in peace with himself. Of course we will never know, and I prayed that the Lord would send love and light to him the last time I visited him in the hospital.

There I was, a failure, beside myself because all of my principles were shattered. I blew it and I really wanted to get away. Eleven thirty that same morning, the telephone rang. It was the V.A. clinic in Cambridge. They wanted to know if I had an empty bed and could take an elderly man. He was in a wheel chair, had sight problems, had to be cleaned up. He only needed shelter for one or two nights, until they could get him into the V.A. hospital at Perry Point.

You've got to be kidding. Yes, I had an empty bed, but I don't need anymore aggravation. NO, NO, NO, echoed in my mind, but my mouth said "sure". I went over to pick him up. He was a very nice, kind and courteous person. My afternoon and evening were spent helping him shower and shave and settle into a bed. After each service I performed, he said thank you. The usual reply I give to persons who thank me is "Don't thank me, thank the Lord. He sent me here." I did not say this all day. Probably an aftermath of the morning. At bed time, I helped him into bed and tucked him in. He said, as usual, thank you. I replied in my normal way, "don't thank me, thank the Lord." As I went to move away, he put his hand on my shoulder and said, "I am". A warm flow of energy passed through my body that resulted in goose bumps. I realized that the Lord was telling me that it was alright to be human and to knock off the self pity. It was my call to continue with all of my faults. I was thankful and honestly I thought that the inference that this man gave me was that he could see the Christ in me. That was wonderful. I could ask for no greater compliment. A year and a half later, when I was discussing this story with my spiritual director, it occurred to me that these were the works of God's description of himself. WOW! Tell me there are not angels for us ordinary folk.

The Lord recognized that if I was left alone to wallow in my self pity, perceived failure and guilt, in what seems to us humans to be a thankless job, I might have packed it in. Who knows? It turned out to be very important in the weeks that followed. The person who left the house had called a number of people and Social Services from the hospital and tell them that I had beat him up. Of course, Social Services had to investigate and he admitted I had only used the pillow to turn his head. Of course, I was annoyed at him for doing this, but I was more annoyed at those persons who 1) believed him and 2) never thought to find out how I was if they could help. Thank God for the love shown at this time because it didn't seem to be coming from anywhere else.

Two weeks earlier his mom came to visit us. We had a room available for her to help her spend more time with him. After the first day she went to a hotel.

She asked me how I could put up with his aggressive personality and downright disrespect. She left two days earlier then planned. The day after the incident. She called me and told me she would sue the Community for abusing her son. Once the investigation was over we never heard from her again.

I'm presenting this as an indication of how the Lord has added love in all episodes during this mission and strength to perform.

CHAPTER 4
THE REAL ESTATE

There is a woman on the phone who would like to speak to you about real estate. "Where is she from left field?" Ha ha. That's quite a joke. Can I have your name? She had a very pleasant voice. She stated "I understand you're looking to buy a house. "No, I have no intention of buying a house here in Cambridge. If I were to buy one I would probably spend the rest of my life in this town." She was not listening and just continued "I will give you a deal you cannot refuse. I have delved with the state government for a number of years. I can show you how to get interest free mortgages, low rate loans and other good benefits. Why don't you just take a trip over to 608 Locust Street .... .like right now". Okay. I'll be there in 10 minutes.

Once again I was quite surprised. The house was three stories high, in fairly good shape and a very good neighborhood. The owner was standing in the doorway and invited me in.

The first floor had a good-sized living room and dining room and a good-sized kitchen. The second floor had three very good-sized bedrooms and one small (Franciscan size bedroom). The third floor is just an attic. There were some indications that maintenance work had to be done, but in general, the house in good shape. I still maintained my mental attitude. Although I had faith she could get me an excellent mortgages. I took one more quick walk through the house and told the woman I will probably be in Cambridge for the rest of my life. The next day we went to the state government, and the house was available to me in two weeks.

There was a social ongoing war with this HIV/AIDS illness It revolved around the fact that the majority of those infected were "gay men". Most of these people were either poor or eccentric. This group had a great deal of trouble acquiring places to live. We organized this house to favor the idiosyncrasy that would come with the vivid life style. A friend of mine, named Dennis, whom 1 met about a year before, was willing to run the house. He was flamboyant and obsessive compulsive. Almost all of the other applicants had similar features which caused conflict. We had to change our philosophy within the next two months back to requiring HIV/ AIDS infection only. The other peripheral aspects were reviewed on an equal basis.

The "Swish" came in and here comes another challenge. My friend Dennis is gone. This leaves me in charge of two houses. Needless to say this was getting difficult. The Friday afternoon that Dennis left a very nice lady asked if she could talk to me. Of course, I talked with her. She had just gotten back from a tour of Michigan. were she was singing gospel hymns. She was from Cambridge, and was looking for a place to stay. I suggested that she could stay at our house and she could help me with daily management problems. She agreed, but had failed to mention that she had a family with her. Two teenage boys, and her husband. This seemed very unlikely to be successful, but we tried. They confiscated the largest bedroom, and they lived out of that for about four months. In general, it was okay. But since they had a Doberman Pincer that bit my hand, we had to ask them to leave for the safety of our guests. One week prior to them leaving, another young lady came to see me and was told by someone that 1 needed office help. I did. We agreed. She moved in. It was very good, but as usual. there was an exception. She had 21 cats. The Health Department frowned upon it and we had to make an effort to get rid of them.

We started to build the intentional Community of St. Francis as a separate entity. A key person. came to help me. He was a Secular Franciscan named Bill. He and I got into a religious routine, including prayers, hymns and discussions. Everyone in the house was invited to join us, if they wanted to. That was one of the major philosophical points in the community. No one was forced to pray or attend meetings. This eventually turned out to be seven individuals assembling each evening for the Liturgy of the Hours Ritual. Bill was also a very hard worker, tremendously helpful to me in all aspects of directing a house. After being with us for a little while he learned that my philosophy was not the same as his. He felt that Franciscans had absolute authority, and when you are in charge everyone has to do as you say. Eventually, this caused us to separate. I'm very thankful for his help.

There are so many instances that are unique and mind bending that one has to be in a educational position 24 hours each day. It would be impossible to try to tell all of these episodes in this document now. Here's a quick review of some instances.

During the 18 years I have had some volunteers come and help me for a brief time. We hoped they could stay at least six months to a year. It was difficult for them to accept my approach to take care of the downtrodden as Christ indicated we were supposed to. It eventually did force me to close the houses and concentrate on outreach activities. We had accomplished what the Lord wanted. My message coming here is to alert everyone to become active in the word of the Lord. There is a need for ordinary individuals, who accept what Christ has taught and wants to apply them in their daily life. Selling everything and giving it to the poor is not easy. The price is indefinable. Christ is saying "I need someone to show the other way". That is limited enabling and does bring about the proper approach to my Father's kingdom. Reading what He says is difficult, and the circumstances surrounding it have to be adapted to it. I will tell you, there is a guarantee that comes with these things as long as you recognize the love of Christ with your whole being. The next time you're in a session of this nature and you look up and sense a sign that says "one way to re-offender". Just edit it and put it back up the other way and indicate that it is a two-way enabler street. And we are obliged to enhance that certain thing as much in return.

This put us in an additional stream of virtues that have been portrayed in the total Christian atmosphere. It is referred to as Restorative Justice . It relates to the complete transmitting of evil effects by a crime on the congregation. It is the sin committed individually that explodes with in the person, their home and   extended families . This type of violation is portrayed in a number of the stories in this book. It is directly related to Christ's exposure to St. Peter. The outline is commit a crime based on your personal aptitude. Your arrested, put in jail,   serve time, get released and returned to society as a productive citizen. Dos this sound familiar? Most of the incidences I refer to are not universal in nature. There is one that is currently reacting on a national level. I believe it is worth noting for an individual who is wealthy and philosophically advanced. Michael Vick is a professional football player. He is a great example of a complete performer of this moral accomplishment. He performed illegally supporting dog fighting. This had been part of his life. There are laws that protect animals from injury or death. He has a great salary and plenty of talent. He was arrested and put in jail for 5 years. His ability to obey the discipline allowed his term to be reduced to two years. When the decision was made he accelerated his new personality and requested to be returned to play football. The courts and the league officials responded positively and he is back in our society. He is caring for his family and donating money to protect animals from cruelty. This Restorative Justice is presented to relate the principle to a person who has performed it today. A question could exposed. Does Christ accept the inclusion of our protrusion in our justice ? Didn't He insist on mercy?

These activities were not always alive at our tribe. There were two guys who disliked each other. One was a computer expert, the other a talented artist. While we were doing the evening prayers, singing or having discussions, they would be arguing over something that was read or interpreted conservatively. Any events that addressed the current atmosphere could cause the blood pressure to go up. These distractions were so nebulous that there was potential violence. I had to control. This artist's name is Robin. He stayed with the Community for a number of years off and on.

The first night he arrived it was raining. We didn't have any rooms empty so I decided to get a motel room. He looks like Patrick Swayze, dresses like a long coat Texas Ranger, rides a motor cycle and has two dogs. One is a Chesapeake Retriever the other is a Chihuahua named Chico. I had the van, so taking the dogs seemed like a good idea. A second request was for me to stay close behind the motor cycle to hide his tail light because it was not working. and he didn't want to be stopped by the police. That seemed reasonable. We started out. He forgot to tell me that Chico liked to sit in the driver's lap and lick their nose. This kept his head right in front of my eyes so I can not see the wet road. That was a challenge but the motor cycle was doing 60 miles per hour and flew out from in front of me within 2 minutes . He forgot his request. He was already registered when I got to the motel. Pointing out the strain made him smile and say "I am so happy that I will start a new life. That thought made me forget the last four days. Thank you and good night." He laid down on the bed and was asleep in one minute. To his credit he did allot of art work and maintenance when he was at the house or in the area.

The last time he was here there was something new. "Robin, how come you're back? I thought, you agreed to go and start a new life with Christ out on the West Coast. We gave you enough money to support you for three months. Where is the money? I told you when you got the money that after 9 years of COSF support you are being asked to leave. We have sustained you on all levels of homelessness, including living in a woods. You have gotten thousands of dollars from the Community of St. Francis and have been thrown out 8 times. I know sometimes you were sick both mentally and physically but you were still capable of understanding the rules and their consequences".

Listen Matt, I was doing wonderfully out on the West Coast and the Lord came to me and said that I had to come back and protect you from all of these evil people. I'm staying here until you are taken by the Lord. I still have my two dogs and will make arrangements somehow for someone to keep them. I am willing to sleep in the cellar or the attic. If you don't mind, I will be part of your volunteer work group". Listen Robin, I will give you two weeks to get settled and then you'll have to leave. You must avoid confrontation with anyone. Should there be a problem, come and tell me and I will handle it. It is important that you keep your thoughts to your self. Don't listen to the voices in your head, stop drinking and smoking pot.

Four months later, Robin went to the hospital. If you don't you will have to leave. Okay, that's your decision. Returning to the West Coast will be a disaster. Since you made the decision, we will help you as best we can. We just had a van donated to the community. It requires some work, but we can get someone to do it. We will give you money for gasoline and food. The rest is your responsibility. Two months later he was gone. The last I heard from him he was in a very good rehabilitation program and doing well. This made him the highest receiver of support funds from COSF.

The Computer Specialist joined us and he was terrific. His expertise helped handled the office activities very well. He did a terrific job helping raise money for a group called Care and Share. Everything went well. He joined the Community for evening prayers also. He was Catholic . We had open floor inter changes regarding the Bible. The subject was the Our Father. I pointed out that we are indulging ourselves in the prayer when we say "forgive us our trespasses as we forgive those who trespass against us". This interpretation was not accepted because there were some persons he would not forgive. The computerized version was revised and he used his version from then on. He eventually got an apartment of his own but came to visit on the weekend Primarily to get fed. He told me on Friday that he was going New York City to spend some days with a female friend. Sunday morning he was found in the apartment having committed suicide by putting a plastic bag over his head.. No one will ever know why. I've been disturbed over the fact that he was extremely happy on Friday morning and took his own life between Friday evening and Sunday. There must be something I missed. The friend he was going to visit told me that he called her early on Saturday morning and said he was on his way. One other questionable fact was that the bag was off his head on the floor. This fostered an investigation. I do not know the results.

Many other people came to the house and bought a variety of things with them. Some of these things are absolutely law breaking. Other things are similar, but had some mental reservations to help protect them from being thrown out of the house. And there were some situations that blended right in with Christ's teaching on forgiving individuals. Each time it was necessary, putting Christ's Teaching into effect proved successful.

There were two friends who contributed office management services. Mary and Chuck were wonderfully oriented to our daily procedures. Their experience allowed others to spread the Franciscan charisma. Once again, out of nowhere Mary moved to Florida. Chuck lived with us off and on. He had some personal problems with the strange couple but did use the forgiveness theory.

As mentioned before, we had four persons, who ran up bills for the telephones over $5000. Two of them were actually operating under a false pretense. They were led to believe that under the new telephone contract, we had free long-distance telephone calls. One of these persons ran the women's house and had a telephone available to her at all times. The other is one of the longest member \ guest of the Community, who has performed transactions to the extreme on both ends of the spectrum. (Her story is related further on in this book).These individuals literally stayed on the telephone for hours and hours. All four persons have succeeded in adopting a positive way of life.

Two of them are still involved with COSF and we are there whenever they need help. Just to show the proper approach, one of these persons will be included as the perfect example of how Christ can work on a daily basis. That will undoubtedly raise your eyebrow. A third person was a young man who had been homeless for quite some time. His girlfriend had just moved to Canada. The price of calls per minute, was ridiculously high. He was not fully aware of the amount but knew there was something wrong. After I received the telephone bill covering two and a half months, I went up to his room. He was aware that the telephone bill had arrived. When I entered his room he was curled up in the fetal position with his thumb in his mouth and crying. He had his bags packed, and was ready to leave. Obviously he had been through this type of situation before. He was absolutely shocked when I told him he could stay and we would work something out. He stayed 2 years. paid a portion of the bill and he's doing very well now.

The fourth person was exceptional. The father of her child was in prison for a number of years. He was 24, and she was 19. He got transferred from a Maryland prison to a prison in Florida. At this time we had put a technical stop on all Long distance calls, She was smart enough to be able to circumvent the policy through her friends ex-cellmate's family. It took two months for the bills to arrive. When they did, I was disappointed, because she had done quite a bit for the Community of St. Francis. She was an excellent cook. Would help me clean the living area and the office. Her ability to handle some other services like shopping for food was exceptional (and expensive). She apologized indicating that she could not pay any money, and will accept whatever my decision would be. The fact that it was the middle of winter with snow on the ground and freezing temperatures certainly came into evaluation of my decision. We had been in existence long enough to support a person and her child financially. This did not include paying the telephone. My Franciscan philosophy allowed her to stay for 6 months plus. She tried unfortunately, to get back with her boyfriend. She became pregnant and left the man again. She has visited us occasionally and the family is doing well.

For instance, there were two individuals who were introduced to each other at The Community of St. Francis. The gentleman has been friends with us for more than 10 years. He is basically an alcoholic with a whole encyclopedia of illnesses. When he was under the influence of alcohol he would become violent or suicidal. He had been in and out of many rehab programs, prisons, jails and the Community of St. Francis. We would help him get out and start all over again. He was sincere in his attempts to control his problems. He would contact COSF sometimes then attempt suicide.

A run of the mill incident was like this. His girl friend was screaming "Matt, Matt call an ambulance. He has just cut his wrists with a razor blade!" There is blood all, over his bedroom and me. I have his arms all wrapped up but he is still bleeding. heavily". Not again, what is the problem today? This is the third time this year, Has he been drinking? He promised not to when I agreed to let him back in the house. She says. "He was proving to me that this type of action did not bother him in the least. This is ridiculous but I still love him". The ambulance is on its way, let's go upstairs and check it out. We went upstairs, put on rubber gloves, and cleaned up the room. We are now faced with performance of Christ's teaching, according to his response to Peter as to how he was to forgive his brother. Over a 10-year period, we have executed the important attribute of Agape love without using a calculator. This particular type of episode was perpetrated by this individual many times. Each time it happened. I was confronted with a Christ in front of me (a'la St. Mother Teresa of Calcutta). The decisions that were made turned into consideration of the negative things that he has produced. We would create an agreement to avoid all of them in the future and as long as he agreed he could stay at the house.

I continued my tirade. Don't you remember the last time he called at 1:30 in the morning and demanded that I go down to the telephone, one block away from the hospital, because he had cut his wrists and wanted me to be with him when he died. Remember he is the guy who was in prison and wrote the poem using my name. I told him I could not go there because it would be an illegal presence. I could be arrested for not calling the ambulance. He reiterated that he did not want an ambulance and hung up. A very good friend Stuart was there, while I was talking . I asked him to please go and help him. He did but by the time he got there someone had already found him and took him to the hospital. Two days later, he was released because he is intelligent enough to convince physicians he is not mentally ill but the alcohol is a problem and he will go to rehab center. I do give him credit for trying . When he got released he came to the house. We are now able to show him our love. Over the last 10 years he was convicted of violence, thievery, drunkenness and anti-social behavior. This guy is exceptionally handsome. He could be cast as a six foot tall Jesus Christ. He was nationally known for having an affair with his case worker while he was in jail in Baltimore, If I were to count the Franciscan events they would probably surpass 490. These occurrences included times in jail which adds to the expectancy covered by Christ's Teaching. After I explicated the new rules we let him stay here until he got into a rehab program. This action is certainly going to be taken as a negative factor effecting his ability to continue to live here.

The woman is a wonderfully loving individual. She is constantly helping everyone she comes in contact with, including me at the house. The two met as a caregiver and patient and fell in love. The doctor told us that he had a month to live. They asked if they could live together in her single room at our house. I felt we were again being given a circumstance to show the love of Christ. They have been living together for a year or more. and in my mind it is not a very happy relationship. They're satisfied. This is a modified success. It is noted and I go on to my next situation.

The next loving event is we have another couple who came to the Community of St. Francis Hospitality House separately. They just basically became good friends. When we closed down the houses they got together, got married and are having a very good time. Their relationship is terrific. COSF gets another high score. Notice how there is not a long related story to go along with this couple. When ever I revisit Cambridge they accept me a their guest. A wonderful return of love.

I have a universal circumstance where my best friend ,who is presented later on, has had all kinds of problems with drugs, men, women and long-distance telephone calls. She has been able to occasionally be successful in controlling her addiction. She and her son's father had problems through the court and the father received custody. My friend went to a rehabilitation program in Atlanta, Georgia. She met a woman down there and fell in love (this requires quite a stretch of love and understanding). Today she is clean, has completed job training, has gotten her legal records expunged, is working in a Rehabilitation Center as a councilor and goes to church, "We just have to love them" A quote from Dorothy Day whom I consider a Saint. I learned a great deal while I was living at the Catholic Worker house for a year.

What am I doing to uplift these individuals? Should I be helping these types of people? Why am I spending so much money to help other people when there are financial debts for COSF ? Just what do you need?. The big accusation is we can enable a person to perform non-acceptable acts. That is the worst thing you can do. If you talk to people in the social services or psychiatric area, you'll find that most of the people say that it's a terrible thing. It could help them once they don't follow through on what you're enabling them to do. You should be blown up in the bomb of whatever their doing, and then the only way they can really survive is to come up the block and join in prayer. Does that sound familiar. There are many, many circumstances where the answer could be, yes. You can use your assets to help them financially, psychologically and rehabilitation wise, to give food. These things can come through, and we will be enabling thousands of people, each one having their own individual problem. This is when they need some kind of help. Somewhere along the line they will be coming directly to us to survive. Setting up a program for enabling is easy. There are some other organizations who give people 3 free bags of food and then tell them not to come back before three-months. There are those who don't have enough money and the group will give them $25 for deposit on a house requiring $400.00 hundred. One method is to tell the person that you have $100.00. If they get $300.00 from others, you will give it to them. What is my path trying to be a true Franciscan? I have the money and you need it. I would give it to you with my supervision. We are talking about hundreds of thousands of dollars traveling through Christ's conduit - The Community of St. Francis Hospitality House.

This brings up a bilateral inquisition. What is the most effective approach to charitable fund distribution.

If you have $100.00 should you give $10.00 to 10 people or all of it to one. This is a dilemma that requires action from the distributor. The major influence is what is the money needed for? If the need is for a deposit on a rented apartment for $600.00 what good is $10.00. However a person may be starving tomorrow so the $ 10.00 could be crucial. The decision has to be analyzed and acted upon according to the loving posture we purport to posses.

There are some people, who we have taken care of for 10 years, off and on. They are fully aware that my justice is based on Christ's teaching. We will start reflecting on, where is the difference between being a loving compassionate person or an enabler. My view is that Christ has very specifically told us that we have to take care of people, regardless of their reaction to us. If we look at Mt 16 24:28 again and see what he is saying, it is difficult to accept. Basically in order to forgive someone 70 X 7 you have to allow them to come back and do something contrary to your lawful understanding. This could result in the person being arrested or put in jail. Christ just tells us that we're supposed to Love without limitation. (Mk 18 28;32 Love your neighbor as yourself) It is not suggesting that we keep a calculator with us to determine when we are to stop showing "Agape" love. We have to show love, compassion and understanding as He has. That means handling, each person with individual dignity and understanding.

This last commentary imaged the type of convergent force that we were introduced to. We were standing in the vestibule of the church waiting for the rest of the procession to join us. We are the Eucharistic ministers. My partner was a very good person. If I were to describe him

to someone I would use the term "pillar of the church" ..
We were in a general conversation when he said he was
very disturbed when the Community of St. Francis moved
into Cambridge. He said he signed a petition not to let
the Community set up shop. I was absolutely shocked,
because I took it personally and knew we did not have
support from our pastor. After I recovered from the shock
of why, 20 years ago, you would not want to experience the
Franciscan Community? Questionably, he said, because he
could see the people you were taking care of as a particular
kind of problem. What definite negative affect the group
would have on the parish. The negative effect on the value
of individual houses in the neighborhood was the major
concern. Overall we did charitable work with the church
but few people knew that. I then asked if they knew what
we were doing,? Delivering love and compassion between
the hospital and the grave was not that obvious. He said"
after a little while, since you were here, we have some idea
that your following Christ. The whole circumstance that
revolves around bringing Francis to Eastern Shore had little
effect. As a tremendous ramifications for the first 12 years.
We really were restricted to people who were sick with
AIDS and poor. Some also were. addicts, homeless and in
many instances, ex-convict. You can see why enabling was
misconstrued.

Once they look at my approach to taking care of
individuals who need help on a one-to-one basis, the
shadow of Mother Teresa could be seen. Dealing with
the crisis as She would, you get into a circumstance that
involves two people. It would be on the outside of the
culture (or should I say inside the temple wall), to start
discussing with me.

CHAPTER 5
SECOND HEAVEN

One Saturday morning our next-door neighbor had a group of people preparing to paint his house. Just in casual conversation. I asked why he decided to paint it now? He said the county investigated the house, which was recorded to be an apartment house. He did not satisfy the measurements, therefore, did not get approval. There were four apartments in the square footage, they did not match the requirements. So he was going to sell the house. As I asked how much he was expecting to get the real estate agent came over to say hello. It was pleasant but nothing really was mentioned about the price. It was obvious that it would take a number of months to get the house ready to be sold. Four months later, the house looked good, and it was an early Saturday morning. My neighbor had told me Thursday night that he was asking $79,000. I said that would be nice. I may be interested in it.

A month later there was a knock on the door, and it was the real estate agent. She said. "I promised that I would give you the first walk-through when the house is ready to be sold." I said, I don't recall that, but I would like to see how well they have improved the house. She handed me the brochure, and I was shocked. They were asking $125,000 for the house. I said no way, but I would like to see the house since he had done so much work. I took three steps into the house turned around and told the real estate agent that if she would give me one day to check out some possibilities for obtaining a mortgage, I will make an offer. She said okay. I went to the state government who had helped us with our current house and they approved. It was fantastic. I had visions of having a campus type operation to help those people in need. After sitting down and discussing some functions with groups from our house, we decided to make the house, a halfway house for individuals getting out of prison. We already had that kind of service as one of our programs. I was walking up the block to see a friend who was a state representative. When I got to her office she had a group of women discussing the problems of the homeless, needy women in Cambridge, Maryland. I stayed for the discussion and was effected by the group. It was a carryover from the experience I had in Washington, DC. Women would rather sleep out in the cold, snow or rain rather than stay at the shelters. There are many abusive actions performed by the men and women causing far more trouble. We met once again with the group, and created an all women's hospitality house.

The Captain of the prison guards at the woman's jail heard about the decision. She took me aside and told me "it is easier to deal with 50 men than 5 woman"

There was some truth in that statement. We had to issue a request for a person to be running the house according to our rules and regulations. The Lord provided us with a wonderful lady, who agreed philosophically and practically with our daily life. The first couple of months were rather hectic. There was a problem with flooding in the area surrounding the town. There were women and children who needed help. Some elderly women did not want to leave their home and were sleeping in their car. Others had to consider their animals and other relatives. We provided the homes for who ever we could. When the crisis was over we reverted back to our original plan. We did allow a priority to a person who was afflicted with AIDS.

The house was beautiful. The first floor had an office, a reception room, a living room, dining room and a kitchen. There was also a full bathroom. The second floor consisted of five-bedrooms and a full bathroom. The third floor had a two-bedroom apartment with a small kitchen and a full bathroom. That was where I was living. The second bedroom was generally used for temporary emergency. It actually offset the daily problems in the neighborhood. We could have as many as nine people in the house. This became difficult to control, although we rarely had that many guests. In general, things went very well for the first year or so.

The house monitor was a good friend of a local pastor and attended her church frequently. The Community of St. Francis emphasized the principle of not demanding persons living in the house to join our religion. She respected this rule in general but started to evangelize each person specifically. She would put up readings from the Bible on each person's door. Verbally indicated that her church and social meetings were mandatory for the people in the house. Some people enjoyed the meetings, but the majority objected to them. Obviously, they complained to me. I re-issued the house rules. There was still a great deal of animosity from the pastor and my friend because I was told that they claimed to be owning the house. Her family got involved and the telephone was still a problem. She needed financial support and a form of none Franciscan dictatorship became prevalent. She was asked to leave.

The group of women living in the house, at this time were getting along well. This opened the possibility of adding the group management of the house. On the surface it worked very well, But on the dark side, many things were going on almost every night. They had boyfriends sneaking in the windows to spend the night. They were usually accompanied by illegal drugs, and/or alcohol. Of course this led to violence, theft and violation of the rights of others. Since our two houses were next to one another, I decided to attempt to run them both. The intention was good, but many of the people took advantage of Christ's instruction (Mk 12 28:32) to "Love your neighbor as your self". This is the major element in the message I'm trying to get across. Our Guests used it to filter the influence of my naiveté approach. My posture had to remain in the shadow of Mother Teresa.

MY BEST FRIEND

My mythical rational was to follow Archbishop Fulton J. Sheen and Jesus Christ by having an ex-Prostitute as a best friend. As mentioned earlier she is a tall, blonde, beautiful body, exceptional looking with a horrendous background. Her name is Dianne and she is very intelligent. Unfortunately, many times this intelligence was used to do things that were illegal.

Dianne came to the door, at 608 Locust Street and asked "may I borrow a cup of cooking oil from you?" "Of course, you may". I gave her a cup and she left. My favorite caseworker from the Department of Social Services, Pat Finley, was at the door with me. I turned to her and said "how come I don't get to take care of the really good looking patients." This is the most notorious statement of "be careful what you ask for". This was about 11 years ago, and we are still in the same process of love and friendship. We try to talk to one another every day, help each other out and show the rest of the world that love is from God through everyone with no strings attached,. I'll just summarize the various emotional and physical events during our friendship.

She was eligible to receive support from the Community of the St. Francis. So we got to see her more frequently. I learned that she had addiction to illegal drugs. This presented a challenge to see how we could get Christ into her heart and help her go straight. We did that. It was precisely what we needed. Then one day she came into the kitchen and mentioned the fact that she was pregnant. She was not living with the father and she needed someone to take care of her and eventually her son. This was an ideal circumstance, for her to stop getting "high". She came to live at the Community of St. Francis and gave up drugs. She did this, primarily for the child. Seven months later, she had a little boy. He was almost two months early. He could barely fit in the palm of my hand. Everything went well in spite of some physical problems. Abortion was never considered. This is why we are such good friends. She handled it very well. But then the old pattern came back and she was asked to leave our house again.

------- FLASH ------

Today's date is April 12, 2008. Dianne has been living with a very good friend that she met in Georgia, about two years ago in a special rehabilitation program. They are unique in nature, which adds to their stress filled lives. They have been doing what is expected of individuals electing to rejoin society without the need of street drugs. This approach is a constant disturbance from all sides of their lives. I just received a phone call. Bad news and good news. Unfortunately, her best friend has been working and received her paycheck last night. That created some reasons to go and get some "crack". This led to her being asked to leave the apartment in order to protect Dianne from being put in the line of fire. I was very disappointed and said a few prayers. About two hours later I received another telephone call from Dianne. She said she had a talk with our mutual friend using my approach. As many times you have forgiven me for violating the rules. You allowed me to come backs after you had thrown me out of the house. I will do it your way. My personality will find it difficult to allow her to stay here for another two weeks. As long as she stays away from her group of friends, she could stay and be more interesting. They did not let it get past the first stage but it was great having the Lord use my simple existence as an incentive.

----BACK TO THE STORY.---

It seems like the stories I am relating to are just routine ways of living. It's very simple to leave put the words on paper, and not bother educating ourselves in order to help. Just a simple night you do some reflection on what actually happened in these situations. How it relates to those around them, and the ultimate dynamic effect on their lives.

Her typical "drugie" event, would be like this. It is a beautiful warm Saturday night. We're all sitting on the back steps of the house after finishing dinner and cleaned the kitchen. Dianne is nicely clothed in a beautiful summer outfit. Everything is matching down to the ribbon on her sandals. She looked beautiful, and everyone mentioned it. Since we are not allowed to have alcohol or drugs in the house, it was not unusual for a person to go for a walk and to come back 15 or 20 minutes later with a slightly different attitude. Most people who smoke cigarettes used that as an excuse to be away for a short time. They were only allowed to smoke cigarettes at a particular designated area. Sometimes we have people who would just come over and visit. Some were just being friendly, while others were casing the joint for things to help them with their addiction. In most instances it was just looking to steal something that would provide relief from their anxiety. It would be anything over five dollars, up to around 35 or $40. On rare occasions an expensive item would be missing. This was expected because everyone knows the tremendous strength of the addictions power.

We hang around having conversations or tell a joke session and possibly having something to snack on. At about 10 o'clock, the group starts to break up, and maybe one or two hang around a little while longer. Many times my good friend and beautiful blonde would stay longer than most. A person from the outside and looking in at that would think of that as being complimentary. It was to some degree. Now I was the person who had charge of the three cars owned by the community. I would go to bed around 10:30. My sleeping quarters were on the third floor in a converted attic. Needless to say once I was up there I could only be disturbed by very loud noises. Those noises were not uncommon, but it was the lack of noise that cause the most problem. My adopted daughter used tremendous intelligence when it came to disrupting our society. She would wait around a few minutes to see if I was praying or was asleep. Once that was determined she had her own car key made, contrary to my knowledge, and she would take a car and head for Baltimore, Maryland. Needless to say the drug "HOOD" was the objective. I would come down around eight o'clock in the morning and she would be looking tired.

You may wonder where she got her money. This is one of the silly Jersey Cityite naïveté psychology principles. After we had been together for a couple of months. We had discussed this particular object. Very simply, she stated, I am a prostitute or you could call me a woman of the night. My reaction was very difficult to understand. No you are not you are an addict. We were sitting in the car. She turned to me, and she said, a prostitute has sex with a man or a woman, gets money, according to the services rendered and then goes on about life. There are times where you can get hundreds of dollars for service or when you can only get a "dime" for a bag of "crack"($10.00). Depending on how deeply you have been dragged down. The difference is as an addict you wind up using the money to buy dope only. There is no difference. Along with the option of selling their body an addict would also be more prone to steal in order to get more money to satisfy their compulsion. The depth of knowledge surrounding ways to illegally obtain money is phenomenal. The addict will steal checks, credit cards, money orders, food stamps and forge signatures on each instrument. This is why many of my friends wind up in jail. Dianne used all of these methods but I never had her arrested. Some times other people would and she would wind up in jail.

Getting back to our relationship, she stated that she will consider me her father. Both spiritually and physically therefore, we will never have sex. I agreed with her. To this day we speak to one another daily and end our conversation with "I love you". The fact taht in more than 25 years I haven't had sex, shows God has helped me to be better. Another aspect that won't be known is that she's dressed extremely attractive therefore she didn't spend all of her money on dope. She keeps in contact with her son on a weekly basis. This major factor has given her the strength to work hard to reverse the malignant life style. I give Christ credit and thanks. As mentioned before, she has been drug free for a year plus. She has a nursing license and now has a job at a Rehabilitation Center as a councilor and a nursing home. Church attendance, participating in local support meetings and bringing the Franciscan charisma with her all day long is wonderful. She is showing how it works.

THE MAGNIFICENT NOISE

Thump, thump, thump it is April 06 2006. We had just finished cleaning up after breakfast when I heard what sounded like a knock on door. The porch usually has a person or two who need our help waiting. I asked the person who was helping me clean to go to the office and tell the people who were waiting that I would be out in five minutes, because I had to make a telephone call. Ironically, the telephone call was to the bank about improving our mortgage situation. The next sound I heard was the thumping of running feet and a voice yelling "it's the Sheriff or his Deputy. He has been here before". I asked "what does he want and who is with him"? As I was walking through the door the Deputy put the hammer in his belt. He pointed to the notice he had nailed and read it to me.

It said this house was sold for back taxes. I clenched my face in disbelief and said this is impossible we are tax-exempt. The deputy stepped off the porch and said "I'm sorry. I am just doing my job. Good luck". I turned and read the complete notice. It stated that the house was sold, because the tax charges were not paid for the first 14 months after we had purchased the house. This was ridiculous for a number of reasons. The first being the fact that the Community of St. Francis is tax exempt. It is officially recorded for a residence that was purchased in 1994. There were numerous other official documents with this notation on them, including tax record in Dorchester County. Needless to say I acted immediately.

After going through many government agencies. We found out that there were many errors throughout the entire system. The first was simply the fact that we should have submitted a form the size of a post card on the day we purchased the house. The flood of errors started right there. We did not receive tax notices because the address on the record was wrong in two places at the County office and a third at the city office. Our houses are in the middle of Cambridge one block away from downtown. How citizens and or government employees could allow the notices to be ignored, should be questioned. Theoretically, there is supposed to be an announcement about the house for sale in the local paper, but no one friend or foe, could find a copy.

The most important requirement was that the person or the company who owns the house before hand, had to pay the taxes. Also any expense that the current buyer had to spend had to be replaced. The person who purchased a house was a lawyer, who lived in the Northeast section of Maryland. This is quite a distance from Cambridge. How could he be the only person interested in buying a very expensive house for a couple thousand dollars. It turned out, he apologized for his lack of knowledge, and actually donated some money to help with our loss. The expenses were not completely put aside as the major blunder in the government office. The Government employees that I dealt with were complacent and showed no concern for the errors on the records or our financial problems. We went, before the Dorchester County council and the city management. A female member of the Council spent five minutes lauding us with praise and respect for the work we did. Then the others acknowledge the importance of our work for all the good we were doing and acknowledge the value of our services. However, none of them suggested that we be excused from paying the taxes. One of the more joyful actions came from a friend who is on the council. He donated the total amount of taxes owed to the city. (This was totally Franciscan which means he is included on our daily prayer list).Four other members of the council promised to donate money. Then did not, but we still pray for them.

Occasionally reviewing the things that have happened, I wonder if there is a specific reason for the entire "off track" process working for four years There was no participation by a single person anywhere until the house was actually sold in a remote area. It was a ridiculously low price and should have been acted upon earlier. Maybe the object was to force a true Christian community out of the neighborhood. Of course, it also allows the aspects of the Lord's spiritual plans to be initiated when necessary. This basically was just the beginning of a number of instances that were completely out of "left field ".

One of the instances I am referring to came about 2:30 in the morning. I was in bed and fast asleep. I was awakened by the sound of a car crashing(a different thump). The safety alarm went off and was loud and very annoying. The noise was directly below my window. However, the street we lived on was one way and I knew my car was properly parked. I stayed in bed trying to ignore the noise. I finally got up and went downstairs. The police had already arrived and there was my car with its rear end up on the sidewalk with another car with it's front end embedded , perpendicular in the trunk area. A witness told the policemen that the car came around the corner, which was five houses away, and claimed he was not speeding. The eye witness could not understand how the driver could get the car In that position. The police agreed and so did I. The driver got out of the car and ran halfway to the corner. A pickup truck came down the street, the driver of the wrecked car jumped into the truck . The truck turned into a parking lot and left the street going the wrong way. It turned out that the car was stolen. The thief was not caught and my car was totaled.

The decision that we had to sell the house was made. The environment was almost identical to my teaming up with Gift of Peace. It was a Friday afternoon around 4 O'clock. I was debating with myself when I heard the "Swish" coming so I rapidly made up my mind to go see our Real Estate Agent on Monday. "Boink" GO NOW. Ok. Our agent was there. We filled out the papers and left. At 10:30 in the morning she called and told me we got two legitimate offers. That was damn near impossible. Only the lord could do that.

Matt Corbliss, S.F.O.

A Noisy Good Friend

There is one person who is the best example of extreme "Agape" application. The Social worker from Worchester County escorted me to the private room in the hospital. She put on a face mask, a robe, rubber gloves and shoe covers. This was a requirement because AIDS was new and was frightening. Of course, I was the rebel who went over and shook hands. I had a pretty good knowledge of transmission prevention and it impressed the ninety eight pound gentleman I was meeting. He had surgery on his brain and that was when they discovered the HIV/AIDS virus. He lived in Salisbury, MD and did not want to go to Cambridge, MD. but the Social Worker insisted. We went. He had a pleasant personality and an infectious laugh. As I picked up his luggage I noticed that he had an unusual package located in his left hand. It consisted of a daily missal three pamphlets with special Memorial prayers. They were all wrapped up with a Holy Rosary. This, of course ,was an indication of his religious posture. He was a Roman Catholic, recently converted . The first of only three active Catholics that we had as guests over the 18 years we were open. That is pretty interesting. He was assigned to a private room because he had shown after effects from the surgery, vomiting and stools. He took his medicine at the proper time every day and he stayed in the room most of the time. He went to mass every weekend, and sometimes during the week. Because of the location of the surgery he had to have a psychological analysis. This revealed a bipolar personality. This problem did not appear for about 3 months.

I was up on the third floor, when I heard a load, angry voice. "you muthafuckin nigabitch. Who the fuck do you think you are talking to. You ass hole--- " as I arrived the offender usually shows respect and calms down. This did not happen. The viciousness accelerated and I was now considered the offender. My experience as a psychiatric specialist in the Army taught me how to handle this type of confrontation, peacefully. It worked. The woman he was talking to was grateful. This type of thing happened about every three months in the beginning. It became more frequent as time went on, This led to a number unfriendly relationships, including his immediate family. His brother hadn't talked to him for years and he only worked three blocks away from our house. His brother came to the house after I spoke with him. When he got to the house he would not go into our Guest's room and within minutes there was a shouting match. That of course just added to the negative tally. As our services expanded, there were many more instances that had violence in the atmosphere. The guy left the house twice on his own. Both instances were disaster. People where stealing money from him. He knows nothing about banking or keeping his apartment clean or protecting his independence card. Each time I had to go rescue him. The Department of Social Services is responsible for protecting individuals that they are supporting. The situation became so negative that this individual was calling up DSS every day reporting on any negative incident even after he left the house. This eventually built a case the Social Services had to address. The investigation was fair but the conclusion was unacceptable. The major requirement was to have certain individuals leave the house, immediately. Even though they did not have some one to replace them. This was not only contrary to my religious philosophy of caring for the homeless but also denied thousands of dollars per month from the government program we were currently involved in. Basically, we allowed individuals to stay as long as they promised to help by paying a stipend that was as much and they couldn't afford. It worked for about two months. From that point on people refused to pay assuming we would not throw them out on the street. Our entire operation had to be closed within the next year.

The point I am making is that we found an individual who was seriously ill, provided him with love, compassion, and understanding' This included caregivers, a home, food, transportation, and access to the Cambridge services. He had legal protection and all the other things that make a good community. He performed his religious functions when it was helpful and he was feeling well. The problems came when he was butting in on someone else's life. These transactions where outside of the demands of his religion and daily life. These were absolutely shocking. This meant we had to deal with both the good and the bad according to Christ's instructions.. He knows I love him in the "Agape" sense and will never end our friendship. I enjoyed our relationship and helped him occasionally in financial situations.

The panorama of this fellow's life, while living with the Community of St. Francis covered all of two way enabling. This something was destined to keep our Community back in our universal houses. We help him to live a good life. Because many aggressive confrontation, both with our guests and other people in the town, we had to close the houses. This was because almost everything that was reported on was questionable and had no supporting documents. He had no business authority. Going around our reporting system and informing any one who would listen, he buried us. What he revealed, could be true or false. All of this involves a man and Franciscan "Agape" love. Just recently I attended a concert in Cambridge, Maryland. I met him. He was bragging about his physical condition and the improved medicine he is taking and his daily life. These are all of the usual things we would talk about. This is the best example of how we were the positive enablers for more than a 10 year period. It started out as a desperate health circumstance, and through the existence of the Community of St. Francis it has been the dwelling place for this individual who can remain open to the possibility of Christ remaining in this life and continuing to growing in love.

Why am I mentioning these events? Because there seems to be a pattern of activities that are performing in the background of which we are not aware. The approach seems to be testing our trust in Christ while our lives are losing our worldly stature. The context of my view is basically three months before the car incident the community had three cars. As of that morning , we had none. We had already sold our first house and now we are in the process of selling the second. We had a wonderful journey, going up the glorious mountain. We are now entering a position, going down the other side of the mountain on a tremendously slippery path. We now have to answer the simple question. What does God want us to do using the glorious gift?

What was the question?

The condensation of 25 years hopefully added to your intelligence reservoir. The umbrella effect revolves around the existence of every thing which is God. Christ has shown us the way to the next plateau and how to love to get there. The answer is in you. Christ's love will show you the way. Just keep listening for the "SWISH"

CHAPTER 6
VATICAN II BASIC

"Forgive them Father, for they do not know what they are doing"

This is an enormously loving prayer . It is generally interpreted as a direct relationship to those who are crucifying Christ. If one goes back over three years of Christ's public life it becomes known that forgiveness is essential to every loving relationship. The principle is applied throughout the variety of wrongdoings that we are being taught how to handle. In our current days we can easily see circumstances where this prayer should be repeated. Some of the major subjects addressed by the churches authority seems to eliminate the third and fourth action. It does not complete the important follow up transactions.

The infiltrated item in most of the events mentioned throughout this book, have one common glaze. Some thing has been stolen from the Community of St. Francis . Each step had to be approached and acted upon in a singular fashion. The administrator has to find out incidentals, approach the transgressor, discussed the circumstance and act accordingly. Forgiveness would be the second essential factor. This should be followed by some type of redemptive service. Once this has been reviewed and the expected results have been specified, and performed the event has ended. The person is forgiven and welcome back to the community. If necessary some changes to help the individual from being tempted should be established and life goes on. The ratification of this event does not eliminate an individual from our group. Even if the same event occurred one hour later, the same process will be applied. Under no circumstances did Christ forgive someone and then throw them out of His church per se.

The Catholic church administration has put that in writing (Vatican Council II). The importance of one following their conscience. It's just stated in the declaration on human freedom in Vatican II the right of the individual.

Man has been made by God to participate in the divine law. Everyman has the duty and therefore the right to seek truth in religious matters. In order to form for themselves true judgment of conscience. This involves seeking truth, according to his human dignity and social nature, through instruction and discussion. When truth is discovered it is held by personal assent. Man is bound to follow his conscience in order to come to God. He cannot be forced to act contrary to his conscience nor restrained from action according to it.

The exercise of religion, of it's very nature, consists for all else in the world. It is an internal, voluntary and free act whereby humans set the course of their life directly toward God. No merely human power can either command or prohibit acts of this kind.

Question 1. Why is Christ advocating the rejection of our current laws by insisting on absorbing the super natural love of the Father?

The key subject in Chapter 2 is the existence of higher level of spiritual creatures which we will be incorporated into us when we die. Our presence in the universe will demand a more total loving emotion. Christ is showing us a "preview of coming attractions". Our problem is we are so influenced by this society that the majority of those born are taught by non -devoted staff (relatives). Secondarily, Christians, in general, do not teach the Love principle from the very first Nowment. There are some wonderful members who live lovingly and convey this to the children. I see the message that the Father is expecting children to be born into a perfectly loving society. Thus by the age of 3 years they are still innocent. It also requires that the functional activities are produced "not by words but by our example". We can verify this by looking at the lives of our Saints (Mother Teresa, Padre Pio, St. Francis.). They owned nothing and followed Christ by helping others. This is exactly what was defined. At this time we do not have the posture to put every one in the saintly group, including your family. This requires a great connection to the Blessed Trinity. All three have an influence to assure there is only one type of loving relationships.

The objective is to have a perfectly loving society without sin. Based on my observance, there is a multitude of spiritual plateaus that remain attainable through Christ's presence. It is up to us to recognize the information given and mold it into the Agape network. Then transport it with my transient self to the next plateau. (I wonder how many trillions nowments it will take). I believe our heavenly existence will be in a unit that exists as a node on a network that is far more functional in speed, identification and transference as we are now. The construction of this unit will provide the communication required to evangelize the bringing of everything into the one loving God. DNA , chromosomes or stem cells are an example of how this process would work. The cognition of this element would be imagining a genius alive in the year 1850 and trying to identify some one using the AT&T methods. It existed but far from earthlings knowledge. We have to listen and implant the method of loving in our minds.

Question 2. How does one provoke a conscientious study of the multiple regulations within the Catholic Church?

Accepting the fact that each person has the mechanism within there being that indicates whether a certain action is right or wrong. This involves a degree of intelligence, which will dictate what action should be taken. When the person reacts contrary to their affirmation it will usually be considered a sin. However, the mental exposure could be thwarted by an action that can be considered equally as important to other people.

An example of this would be Oswald deciding to kill JFK, the president, for a group of foreign politicians. Or the terrorists acting on Sept 11 2001(There is a poem relating to this event on page?//)When this takes place the assassin is a criminal killer to the citizens of that country. However, he is a national hero to the country that authorized him. His decision was effected by his debating to arrive at the conclusion. Your conscience is an intricate part of your body and soul. It is activated during all transactions that you are performing. This comment is just related to religion.

The methodology installed to investigate the prolific rules and regulations of your current church would be a procedure for comparing them to other religions. Once you have completed the comparison study, you would then understand the differences in your decision. You're election would be based on your conclusion. Many times during an educational presentation, I have stated that I have studied a number of religions and have concluded that the Catholic Church is the one true Church. If in the future I gain some information that convinced me that there is another religion more effective than my church, I would be obliged to join that church due to my conscience.

The Catholic church administration has put that in writing (Vatican Council II). the importance of one following their conscience. It's just stated in the declaration on human freedom is the right of the individual. It is written:

THE RIGHT OF THE INDIVIDUAL.

Human beings have been made by God to participate in the divine law, Every man and woman has the duty and therefore the right to seek truth in religious matters. In order to form for themselves true judgment of conscience, seeking truth, according to their human dignity is essential. It is attainable in social nature, through instruction and discussion. When truth is discovered that is held by personal assent the human is bound to follow his conscience in order to come to God. He can not be forced to act contrary to his conscience nor restrained from action according to it.

The exercise of religion, of it's very nature, consists for all else in the world. It is an internal, voluntary and free act whereby humans set the course of their life directly toward God. No merely human power can either command or prohibit acts of this kind.

The social nature of man requires that he give external expression to his internal acts of religion.

We now have to answer the simple question. What does God want us to do using the glorious gift.

Here is another conscience laden events that are related to the Community Hospitality House. There were many more incidences with the same type action but with a different cast. However there is one character who fulfills all aspects of portraying the issuance of our Agape Love involving non-abortion.

We had a young lady who was 18 years old, and two months pregnant. Her position was the victim of three other girls beating her up. The reason because of her relationship with a "Niga". This conflict was being held on our porch as I pulled up my car. When I got out of the car, the three girls attacked me but change their mind when I didn't run away. They were screaming vulgar language, threats of violence and then throwing beer bottles in the street. Of course, this made our neighbors very happy. I escorted, the young lady into the house and had a conversation. Her boyfriend had thrown her out of his house and she had nowhere else to go. I allowed her to stay for the night. Her boyfriend put her cloths out on the street. She asked if we could go and help her pick them up. When we got to the house there was a young man standing by her wardrobe. She introduced me to him stating he was her best friend. We took her cloths and went back to the house. The following evening, she came back at dinner time and had a young man with her. She introduced him to me as her best friend. I asked, what happened to her best friend last night? She just said, He is gone.

A short time later, I was taking my best friend home from jail at 12 o'clock midnight. There was a "gangsta" walking out the driveway. She recognized him because he was also just released. We offered him a ride into town. He was grateful and went his way. Three months later, that black stud, who we gave a lift from jail, came to the house to visit the young lady. She was pregnant with his child. It was his 16th child and he did not support any of them. He was very harsh and violent attempting to prevent her from doing drugs while she was pregnant. This was almost a daily confrontation. Both of them spent some time in jail before the baby was born. In between he was crawling in the window by the office at our house and spending the night with her. Eventually, someone let me know what was going on and I had them leave. We still supported her with food.

This brings us back to our young girl. She had her baby in the town next to Cambridge. Her boy friend didn't have any transportation so I drove him up to the hospital to visit her. When we got there we met, a policeman and a man and two women. They were all part of her family. John just happens to be an African-American. Her family had legal action to prevent him from seeing the baby. This accelerated fast into a confrontation that required the policeman to escort us out of the hospital. Unfortunately, the young lady contracted some disease, and the child was given to John's mother to take care of her. The main reason was they were still on drugs. In most instances, the people at this stage become prostitutes in order to support their addiction. Four months later she was pregnant again. He had just gotten out of jail and the whole process started all over again. After a number of violent incidents he was back in jail. The last time I saw them she was eight months pregnant, and with a woman I knew had addiction problems. They came to visit at one o'clock in the afternoon. We had a short conversation, because I had to go and watch a movie, which would be about 2 ½ hours long. I came back they were still there, and we asked them to stay for dinner. They became nervous and hyper and suddenly decided to leave. About a half hour later, I was in one of the bedrooms with Diane. As I went to sit on the bed she stopped me and told me we had to wash the sheets. I asked why? She said Mary and her friend went out and got two men to come in the house and went upstairs to have sex. When they were finished in less than an hour they went out and got two more.

Two days later, Mary was arrested, and my friend had the baby one month later. This was an insight of situations that we dealt with every day using Christ's teaching as our guide. If she were to go back to me, I would help her as much as I could in the agape mode. Abortion never entered our realm even with the poor results effecting the children.

These are just instances from the thousands we dealt with. There is another story earlier about the individual who I consider my best friend. I felt that abortion was definitely going to be performed. She applied the lessons learned in the wonderful COSF NOW.

CHAPTER 7
MY TURN

Having reviewed the 25 years of my Franciscan ministry, there should be a brief background leading up to the sledgehammer swing. These are my views on some of the things I believe are general questions from particular individuals who are converting to Catholicism. My experience as a conveyor of our mortal position involves the seventeen years of Catholic school. I was accepted in the Third Order of Saint Francis in June 16,1956. Along with being a Franciscan Formation Director, Retreat Master, Author & Presenter I worked with the parish. General it involved teaching RCIA, CCD, Bible study, renew groups. This involved living as a loving father and a humble servant. Employment in the computer industry was pursued to support my family. As mentioned earlier, the relationship with God started when I was nine years old. I was infected with polio. It is known as Bulbar polio which affects your throat and breathing. Very few individuals survive the initial attack. The Lord had a different idea. This was my first indication that there was something floating around in the spiritual world. Why did I think that? While I was in bed for five weeks, I had unusual exposure to some religious principles. My mother and sisters were praying for me. My dad died when I was nine. This meant that mom, Saint Clair, (mom) had to support the children. She had no business experience. Moping the floors in a public high school was the only job she could get. Her political influence was through Monsignor Leroy McWilliams. He authored the book "The Parish Priest". Obviously she did well and wound up being a librarian in the same school. St. Anthony became the patron saint of our family. Included in this book is a copy of the families love. All of this revolves around the first acknowledgment of the love of God. After a number of days in an iron lung and the rest of time in a room by my self, I was able to recognize the results of heaven, hell, and purgatory. Then recognizing basic factors, I started to pray for the Devil. Why? Because I didn't accept the fact that my loving Father would condemn anyone to stay in hell forever. Was I Anti-excommunication at that early stage?

THE JOURNEY -B. C.

You should note that B. C. is only the abbreviation, because Christ has been with his servant from early childhood. There was a love present in two other Third Order Franciscans who were Saintly parents, Clair and Joseph Corbliss. This was not recognized until "the call." became loud and clear. They had four children. Three girls and a guy. The three girls were excellent Catholics. The eldest was a Mother Seton Sister of Charity with the Franciscan family connection being her name, Sister

Marie Anthony. The other two sisters, Marilyn and Lucille were natural saints raising families of six and seven children.

The schooling provided the servant was all Catholic through the fourth year of college. Some might question the statement since he went to Saint Peter's College in Jersey City N.J. which was run by the Jesuits. However, to offset the influence of Saint Thomas Aquinas, the Lord had the servant professed as a member of the Third Order of St. Francis . This preceded my marriage and my college-level schooling. Marriage came first, then the education. We were blessed with seven wonderful children. We now have 28 grand children and three great grand kids. My wife deserves kudos for encouraging me to attend an experimental night school program that issued a diploma in 4 ½ years. This curriculum was applied while working a full-time job. This required more time from her to raise the family. This also required that I help her in every parenthood action dictated to this wonderful family. She spent more time with the children then I did. The "call" to serve was definitely involved in raising a family, along with the peripheral activities. These included Catholic parenting, schooling for the children, parish and social activity and employment. When all of the children were in school my wife, Barbara, went to nursing school and graduated . After 31 years we took a good look at where we were and our future. My wife and I decided to separate amicably . After all of the children were on their own and I was involved in the worldly pursuit of wealth. It was then that the "call "came. The "call" was there all along as a light whisper, while I prepared breakfast every Sunday morning for the family. This began when I was an altar boy, and served 6:30 mass. It was just as a whisper " you are here to serve ". I accepted that and served breakfast. I also accepted that the Lord might want me to be involved in the pursuit of worldly influence through my own company. These were both given up. The call now came with the power of the sledgehammer "YOU ARE HERE TO SERVE". I said, I thought I was serving God.

Nope, Nope, Nope!

It became clear that one could not follow Christ or St. Francis and continue to devote the vast majority of their time to" Mammon" (business). It also became clear that I was to devote all my time to serving Christ, through loving care of the Poor. This revelation was wonderful, except that I was not sure how to do it. That may sound strange for someone who has been an integral part of many Catholic institutions and the parishes (does that tell you something). The position that Fr. Duggan had given me was much too comfortable. The transition from the business world was made so smoothly that I felt working for Christ in this capacity was a dream. This was a joyful way to attain heaven. Right?

Nope, Nope, Nope!

The "call" had a few words added to it. " THE POOR" . The parish I worked in was not known for its ghettoes. It was rather affluent . The Message from Ducky the dinosaur, of Hollywood fame, is just to let us know that this message is here "before our time"..

The polio effect is still present in my throat after 65 years. Recently I have been unable to swallow at all. This is a loving acceptance of God's will. We had gone through a tremendous amount of mortal activity that challenged my trust in Christ. So far, so good. As you will see there is allot of miracle interference as life progressed. Just one visit by an angel back in 1945. My mom's Family were having a picnic at a lake in New Jersey. The swimming area was designated by ropes and poles. A young child threw an inflated plastic ball over the rope. I thought that it was easy to retrieve, so I went under the rope and swam after it. Each time my hand entered the water it caused a wave that pushed the ball further away. When I got a long distance away from the rope, I got a mouth full of water and began to choke. (this was about a year after the polio struck) I panicked. My arms were flurrying and they hit something that I could hold onto. It was a man sitting in a large black car tube . He just told me to hold on and catch my breath. I did. The ball had continued to the other side. There was allot of noise coming from the beach, but I was anxiously swimming to get to the beach, so the noise meant nothing. As the rope was within my reach the Life Guard grabbed me and carried me to my family. My mom was crying. Everyone else was highly disturbed. My uncle Frank yelled at me and wanted to know "why was I out there and how did I survive"? It looked like I was drowning . I was pointing out to where the man in the big black tube was and I told him what happened. He looked out there and there was no one on the lake. He said "you were just splashing in the water. My answer was that I wasn't dreaming. As my uncle walked away, the Life Guard bent over and said "son, we do not allow that type of tube in this lake. (Da dida da daa)

The most important operation was a quadruple bypass of the heart.

It was March 14 1997 me and my dog were out during the evening stroll. I felt a pain in my chest, but it went away, as it does every night. I always attribute it to a form of angina, which is a carryover from my days of running. However, the pain came back. So when I got home I made a note to have my doctor check it out. We made an appointment for two weeks. That night I went for an evening walk with my dog again, and the pain came back twice as intense. I went to the hospital. My doctor was not in the hospital, but the doctor covering was a friend. She used tests and told me that I had to be admitted to the hospital. I tried to explain to her that my Dog was in the car and he will not let anyone enter it without me being there. She said that I would have to make the arrangements because I have to be in the hospital. We had a slight discussion but I had to sign a paper alleviating the responsibility if something happened between the time I left the hospital took the dog home and got back. I was admitted to the emergency room. There was another friend who was a doctor dealing with the AIDS patients I had been in contact with many doctors, He came in with my other friend and simply asked what hospital did I want to go to? The choice was Georgetown University Hospital nationally noted for its cardiac programs or the Peninsula General Hospital in Salisbury, MD. I chose Georgetown number one, because of its reputation and because my wife, the nurse, worked there. They set me in an ambulance and transported me over the Bay Bridge and up to D.C. with the siren blasting and the lights flashing. At this point, no one had indicated to me what the problem was. They performed a few more tests and came back and told me.

I would probably need an operation known as bypass surgery.

"Now Matt, I want you to know that I have performed this type of surgery hundreds of times. Our success rate is better than 90%. However, I am obliged to tell you that on some circumstances, where things might not go as planned this can result in your death". Do you understand this? My answer was "what's not to understand ? What was not crystal clear, thank God, was how they went about repairing my circulatory system. Cracking open my chest ,as referred to in the movie MASH, became much more realistic. It was MY rib cage they were cracking and re-fixed with wiring. It would be me looking like a mutated octopus with all kinds of tentacles. This could also be me on the table when the doctor shouting "clear' or the doleful siren of a "flat line" indicator trumpeting my departure. We shall see or maybe not.

Surprisingly. My concern was more for the kids. I really did not want them to go through "goodbye" ritual. I still feel that your last happy departure should be loving and joyful. I do not want anyone to be inconvenienced, but the kids never listen to me. This would be ideal for a St. Patrick's day party. Which we generally would have celebrated at an Irish pub. The girls made a general bon voyage wish ,but the boys as macho as they are, wanted private .audiences. This was exactly what I didn't want because I knew I would cry and get all sloppy (I did and each one made me feel wonderful as they expressed there feelings) My original thoughts were wrong. Your family should be there to express their love and concerns. The operation was scheduled for six o'clock in the morning. I actually slept well, although six o'clock came real fast.

"Lay down on your back, spread out your arms also I have to put this on your head. My last thought was "that is probably what they said to Christ". My next conscious thought was, "who is this pretty woman and what are these tubes she has connected to me. My chest was uncomfortable but did not hurt. Thank God for drugs. Have you attempted to analyze a situation? Yes, the vegetarian, marathon running, non-smoking, alcohol free drunkard has survived a quadruple bypass heart operation. Don't go on about the "he doesn't fit the profile or he looked so healthy." fifteen years ago, my main artery was "clear as a bell". These are the exact words from a leading cardiologist. On this March 17, there was only a threadlike passage for the blood. It is now twelve years later, and my heart and mind are still in good shape. We shall not discuss the other parts of my physical being. However the blockage was caused by substituting meat with cheese.

Fortunately, the Lord created a circumstance where my youngest daughter, Cathy, could run the house for a month and a half. This allowed me to have an emergence of a new life with Saint Patrick's feast day as my new birthday. The miracle is the current extra twelve years that I've been able to live.

Most of the other things I am putting in this chapter are evoking subjects that people have specifically asked me to discuss during educational interfaces. These presentations are my interpretations that are available for self education. They can be accepted, rejected or just filed for future reference.

Question 1. Why did the Catholic church change the sacrament of confession to Reconciliation?

Cradle Catholics having very difficult time with the transition from "confession" to "reconciliation". In their minds, the sacrament is the same, so why make a big deal out of it. Confession was definitely easier (although you were sure the priest recognized your voice, thus the strange look when you saw him on Sunday morning) all you had to do was avoid a tough priest, muffle your voice, tell your sins and do the penance given by the priest, usually three Hail Mary's.

Now, "they" want us to actually come face-to-face with the priest, sitting in a lighted room and tell your most intimate secrets. Why? We liked the valued anonymity of confession. The explanation of the new way makes much more sense. The church as a community is physical and present. Christ is the head and body of this physical entity. Any sin deemed committed has a relation to the right of individuals who are members of the church or the social groups in which one lives. The offense, therefore, is against the society in which we live. So, to reconcile means to make friendly gestures. This means to settle , bring into harmony or compose differences within that organization or person. Depending on the nature of the infringement on another's right. one must have either direct contact with the person offended or a representative of the society. When rights are abused, it is an affront to all persons in society. This means that there is a need to return to a normative stature with the person offended and the rest of the crowd.

As church members we have given the authority to the hierarchy in order for them to represent us in matters spiritual and temporal. They are not in our purview as the duty to perform. One of these attributes is as conciliator with the rest of the church. Since he represents the church, he is in major conduct of cumulative actions for us. We express our concerns and views to the priest who is a physical representation of Christ and the church. He physically makes us loving, composed and in harmony with all parties involved. He may suggest that you reconcile directly with the offended party if the situation dictates it. i.e. return stolen money, pay medical bills, etc.

Now that we see the true reconciliation process, which may have a heavy penance ritual attached) we can see that speaking directly to the priests no different than speaking to Christ. The priest is the "legal" representation for both sides.

There have been many instances where we as Christians and/or some representative of our church have erroneously infringed on the rights of others. All but in good conscience. Once this situation is perceived, it is incumbent upon us as the church to reconcile the offense with or without the conduct of priestly authority. If a person has been denied God given rights and led to believe that the love of the Lord is not available to them, then a definite wrong has been committed. This must be reconciled in the name of Christ then the church . This is the physical result of our physical being in concert with our spiritual entity. Since we are dichotomized in nature, our reconciliation must be diametrically complete in nature. to separate into a distinct opposing part.

Question 2. Is FORGIVENESS essentially a part of the loving procedure?

Christ said

"Forgive them Father, for they do not know what they are doing" .

Again, this is an enormously loving prayer. It is generally interpreted as a direct relationship to those who are crucifying Christ. If one goes back over three years of Christ's public life, it becomes known that forgiveness is essential to every loving relationship. The principle is applied throughout the variety of wrongdoings that we are being taught how to handle. In our current days we can easily see circumstances where this prayer should be repeated. Some of the major subjects addressed by the churches authority seems to eliminate the secondary action that is required to complete this important transaction.

As mentioned throughout this book, one common incident is when someone has stolen from the Community of St. Francis. Each step had to be approached and acted upon in a singular fashion. The administrator to find out incidentals, approach the transgressor, discussed the circumstance and act accordingly. Forgiveness would be the essential factor. This should be followed by some type of redemptive service. Once this has been reviewed and the expected results have been specified, the event has ended. The person is forgiven and welcome back of the community. If necessary some changes to help the individual from being tempted should be established and life goes on. The ratification of this event does not eliminate an individual from our group. Even if the same event occurred one hour later, the same process will be applied. Under no circumstances that Christ forgave someone did he throw them out of His house (church) per se.

Question 3: How do you treat a woman who is having an abortion?

Approaching the combination of the principles of these answers ,the current disaster involving abortion is a good portrayal of the various actions. They involve conscience, decision, love, forgiveness and some negative actions,

Twenty years ago, I was taking care of a woman who had two children and was living with AIDS. She had a minimum income, and was living in a house that had a roof that had fallen in. There was no heat or water and no transportation. We did very well together to get the house more livable. Each morning her children went off to school, clean and well dressed. After a couple of weeks. I was told by Social Services not to go to her house anymore. About one month later I met her in a shopping mall. After a brief conversation, she told me that she had an abortion. Since she knew I was Catholic, she assumed I would no longer associate with her. I explained that that was not true we would help her as much as we could. It was her decision so she had to answer to God for it. I did not know she was pregnant, or I would have discussed circumstances and why I consider it murder. However, it would still be her decision and I had nothing to do with it. The point I'm making here is not the millions of children who were killed are human beings and should have human right. This has been well documented. A person like my self may respect the parent's right to make a decision even if it is diametrically opposed to my beliefs. The major effort is to show love to the being that has caused the hassle and relay it to your family, community and parish. The negative actions taken to keep Christ away from those He specifically tells us to love is an abomination. You will be reminded through these pages (70 x 7).

CHAPTER 8
ESSAYS AND POEMS

Written by the Author and his family

The "DADDY" poem was awarded First Place in the Showcase Edition of "A Celebration of Poets". It was written by my youngest Daughter. It ranks with Mother Teresa in my world.

$\mathcal{D}$ADDY

by Cathy Corbliss

He is the beat of my heart;
he is the kindest man I know.

His heart is filled with passion that
was hidden long ago.

He has gone through many changes
since the time that I was young.

He has done so many wonderful
things that will never come undone.

He has taught me so many things in
these last few years.

He has been there all my life,
just to wipe away my tears.

He is the man someone will have to
steal my heart from.

He just can't wait for that someday
to come.

He will miss me when I'm gone;
we are best friends, you know.

He'll always be there for me,
wherever I may go.

DID YOU EVER WONDER ....

If AIDS was the beginning of the end of the world?

About 25 years ago HIV/AIDS became formally identified as a deadly incurable disease. Once diagnosed the life span was a couple of months. At that time the statistics dealt with one hundred thousand persons worldwide. This epidemic cost millions of dollars and a great wave of sorrow. The virus is still not curable. Medicine has improved the life span which is now up to 20 years. It is active in every country and is at a pandemic nature. We have spent billions of dollars, buried millions of people and it is still here. I have been notified that it is expanding again, world wide and our country. The major groups involve gay men, teenagers and individuals over age 60. My major concern involves the teenagers. The statistical category used up to now is ages between 15 and 25. There are equal, if not more children, from 10 to 15 participating in sex. Why am I issuing this article? Because there is a need for education programs focused on the teenage groups in this world. The current material is very good for technical evaluation by professional teachers. The students listen but do not hear.

President Obama signed a bill in April allocating $45 million for supporting programs that are associated with the AIDS virus projects This is a very good approach to supporting the existing battle against the AIDS pandemic that we are facing today. Unfortunately, this total amount is merely incidental to the total amount of attributes that are needed to conquer this disease. There are approximately 56,300 new infections each year in the United States. These statistics are related to information that has been recorded by clients. It is estimated that there are probably an additional 20% more persons who are infected with AIDS and do not know it. This is offset by the fatal results of 14,000 deaths per year. The result leaves 42,300 persons with AIDS (PWA). There are so many features derived from this virus that it would be impossible to attack every one of them here and now. Because of our current economic down fall many agencies are being eliminated or cut back drastically. There will be many more actions of this nature. This aspect of financial requirements for servicing is important. However, extensive education high lighting abstinence from sexual and/or drug behavior is the primary factor that must be emphasized. The health danger caused by the transmission of STD (Sexually Transmitted Diseases) should be taught on the moral and physical level. Teenagers should be the major audience. Most of the statistics emphasize young people between 15 and 25 years of age. The category is valid but, children at the age between 11 and 15 have not only had sex but have gotten HIV/AIDS, pregnant and other STD's.

Educational material is available at every Health Department, Department of Social Services and the Federal Government. The personnel at these agencies will help you on each level of concern. It is your activity that is needed.

I would like to start this article with a parable. There once was a town that was situated in the direct path of the water that flows from an enormous dam. This dam had billions of gallons of water behind it. There was no question that if the dam broke the whole town would be obliterated. No one would escape from the torrential flood without help. The dam broke! As the water approached many people could see it coming and said things like "I told ya'll we should have built the damn dam thing thicker" or "This is all the Governments fault". As they were being swept away in the water some others said "I know what the problem is. You just hold your breath for 1 or 2 years , I'll see if I can repair the damn." Yet another said "I think we will all drown" to which the reply came, "Look we offered free swimming lessons, is it our fault that these people didn't take advantage of them.

There was a group of people who were fortunate enough to be on high ground and they were trying to help. They shouted "there are boats off to your left. It is your only chance". Some people listened and started to swim toward the boats. Others hesitated and were heard to say I don't like the colors involved or it does not meet our specifications. They are made out of rubber . I Think I can make it without rubber protection.

The group on the hill yelled "it is your only hope". There is a bigger wave coming behind this one. Use the boats. They won't fix the dam but they will keep you alive until the problem is solved. Some of those who hesitated became enlightened and accepted the suggestions. Those who did not listen watched their children drowning yelling, "I am telling you not to drown. You listen to me".

This is not one of my favorite stories but it is a lesson that has to be taught. What went through your mind as you read this story? How unintelligent can people be? We can not hold our breath for a long time. It is natural to have to breathe. What has swimming lessons got to do with this spiritual crisis? Why wouldn't everyone use the rubber protection? Who were the people on the hill? I hope you thought of these and many more questions.

It is a simple allegory that has a direct correlation to the situation I found myself in every day. I have been working in multiple communities on the Eastern Shore of Maryland ministering to victims of AIDS for twenty years. I am particularly concerned about our teenagers. The thrust of this concern is the probable effects of Sexually Transmitted Diseases (STD) which includes AIDS. The parable comes to mind because on a daily basis, I encounter people who acknowledge the problem of HIV/AIDS virus. They are aware of the life threatening aspects of it. The approach seems to be irrational about it's effect on their lives. The prevailing attitude seems to be "it will not happen to my family". Maybe, if we don't talk , it will go away.

There are many reasons for this type of reaction. First most parents feel that they have taught there children well, even if they haven't talked about sex and drugs. It is also difficult to believe that our children would always do what we wanted them to do. The family is also absolutely sure that their children are not sexually active because, mom and dad can "sense" those things. Be that as it may, someone's children are making up the statistics that show at a Middle School level as many as 60 out of 100 students are sexually active. These are teens that have volunteered this information in formats that are very reliable. Even if these statistics were not true and were only 25%, I would still be concerned for those 25 students.

Secondly, we have finger pointing. Everyone has a scapegoat. If it is not our society, it's the family unit or television or the churches. We don't teach moral values to our youngsters and they should know that sex is only meaningful in the marriage state. Most of the curriculums include abstinence-only. Very few people say "maybe I am part of the problem". Let me say here that there is no doubt in my mind that the major causes of this problem (Teen Sexuality) is the lack of honest family communications. Parental commitment and the lack of a healthy self esteem influence the network. That fact does not alter the posture of the predominately Christian communities I have been dealing with. We should apply the criteria regarding the saving of our society and our children's lives.

Thirdly, the seeming lack of knowledge of Government officials as to the seriousness of this plague. Each city, county and state has Health Professionals (the Group on the high ground) have been and still are warning us as vociferously as they can. There is printed material from every avenue possible pointing out the devastation that is upon us. There are concerned citizens, who have been pounding on doors to awaken the rest of the neighborhood . Unfortunately, there does not seem to be any reaction. (This is where I hear the foolish comments).

I do not understand this course of action. If I ran into any office and said ·"there is a holdup at the bank and your family is being held hostage. Your family is in danger of being shot. Each person would have temporary heart failure, go running to the bank, find out what they can do to save their family and demand to know what the police are doing. Well I am saying the same thing.

The message is simple

There are no longer specific groups that have exclusive rights to this disease. It is prevalent in all levels of our society. Our main concern is for the sexually active teenager because:

o   They are at a higher risk because their immune system is not fully mature.

o   If they contract AIDS virus they have the life expectancy of 15 years or less

o   As the disease progresses they will need financial assistance, medical attention and prescriptions .

o   When AIDS becomes predominant, the person is generally unemployable because of the frequency of illness and the regimen of clinical visits.

o   In the later stages the victim will require personal attention in a hospital or a home.

o   All of these stages require Government support.

Because of the age of the teenager and their unemployable status, public assistance will be required for a much longer time. This is a major drain on our current government budgets causing massive cutbacks. This financial demand will literally go out of sight.

By now your saying "Get to the point". My point is that we have to recognize this problem as a major catastrophe, here and now. There is no room for finger pointing or moralizing. Most of us have failed our children and we must do something about it, short term and long term.

Let's look at the long term first. All of the Communities have to take a realistic look at how we are teaching the principle of love to our families. Love fosters commitment and compassion both of which are vital to the construction of an unselfish world. We can all get together to start rebuilding the dam.

In the short term we have to protect our children regardless of what the means are. The most important opinions in this scenario is that of our children. We have used up our options and they are not working per the research reports. I have proposed that we provide a forum for our teenagers to express their opinions on the various STD problems. We can use the information obtained to formulate a more meaningful program to educate using their culture. We have to educate everyone to the reality that is present, dangerous and a lethal threat to our children. All parents must learn about the diseases and the effects of teenage pregnancies. Discuss them with your children. I emphasize discuss, not dictate. As the father of seven children, I am disappointed that all of my children do not follow the same path that I believe, but I accept that. Based on this knowledge I can communicate with them on the level that is acceptable to both of us. I used to assume that they all were staunch Catholics and understood everything about doing what is right in the eyes of the church. This was a mistake. It only occurred to me later in life that the church had Reconciliation for me to be forgiven for my mistakes. My children's view of this moral approach is that our children may not have the exact same beliefs or strength of belief as you and me. They are all strong Christians. There is a strong feeling that love will be taught to my 27 Grand Children. This means that for me to rely only on the Roman Catholic Church teachings or the bible for authority is futile.

Find out what your children believe and understand. This can give you an awareness as to how you can help them avoid disaster for their physical well being. You can also direct their spiritual growth according to their progress. This will bring you closer together, show that you love them. You accept them as a person and give you mutual ground to build a more loving family structure. Remember that you cannot dictate or legislate love. You can only live it and it will come back tenfold plus. Try it, you will like it.

Please, please, please listen to your health officials. Start to rebuild the family unit into the wonderful existence it is supposed to be through your love and your community. Above all listen to your children and love them even if you do not agree with their position. You cannot force someone to build a house if they haven't the slightest idea about the material to be used. Your definition of the roof structure is useless if the person you are trying to help is still struggling with the concept of cinder blocks .

We are all in this together, so let's put the safety of our children and our community ahead of our personal prejudices. We must all strive to restore the true value of moral principles and loving one another. We cannot let those who are in physical danger die because we didn't and are still not doing our job.

DID YOU EVER WONDER ....

if Christ meant what He said about the "Rich"

Recently, at a youth gathering, a young man asked me "what was wrong with having a million dollars?" Once again I fell back on an old cliche" "Money doesn't make you happy". I know the answer bothered me because it did not impress this youngster attitude. After much consideration I realized that an abundance of wealth is contrary to Christ's nature and humanity. If God wanted there to be a "de facto" separation between\ us regarding wealth, we would be born with some" article" of wealth attached to us. This has never happened. It only after birth that, based on the position of our percent, we can acquire the benefits of what our society calls wealth. We" profess that all human beings are created equal and then spend the rest of our living be better then someone else. Christ had no possessions and advocated loving one another. How can we be like Him? He asks, and has an excess of possessions and exclude others from our lives and the gifts we have received. Humanity itself demands equality of rights and living conditions. The lack of true love, allows greed and avarice to eliminate this quality.

Oh yes, there will be some very strong reactions to this analysis of the words of Christ, However, it is long overdue. If the total condition of our society is not openly reviewed and discussed there is little hope. The cancer that is eating away at our world is within all of us and we are feeding it with our own greed. One person stated that they could not believe that God could be that judgmental. Most of the people we know, our families and friends will be lost if that were true. BINGO. That is exactly what Christ was warning about. This is not an interpretation of some words. It is not something that leads one to misunderstand. These are straight forward words that were written by all three Evangelists. Christ does not correct any misconception on the part of Apostles, as He did frequently in other areas. Immediately after Christ makes this statement He assures Peter and the others that they will have eternal life for the things they have given up for Him. Lk 18:29-30) There can be no question that Jesus meant what He said.

So, what if it is irresponsible for everyone to being self centered. Few people are going to give up a spacious house, cars, etc. and follow Christ. Do you feel this is just another scare tactic to make us think? Is this even stronger? There is a distinct appreciation for how St. John the Baptist felt as he stood in front of Herod accusing him of being wicked and urging him to repent). Each of us has to listen to the message that is uniquely transmitted to us individually by the Holy Spirit and pray.

Yes, those of us that fit in the category of rich, all agree that it is impossible for us to enter the Kingdom of God if we have to ride that small camel. Is there any Hope? Of' course, in that same passage Jesus says "that is impossibl€" for human beings but is possible for God. II Lk (18:27) ". A rich young ruler asked him "good teacher, what must I do to inherit eternal life? "Why do you call me good?" Jesus asked him. no one is good but, One-God. You know the Commandments:

Do not commit adultery; do not murder; do not steal; does not bear false witness; honor your father and mother."

"I have kept all these from my youth" when Jesus heard this he told him "you still lack one thing: sell all that you have and distribute it to the poor, you will have treasure in heaven. Then come ,follow me."

"Whew! That's better. Or is it? We are being told directly again by Christ and we are in trouble. We still want to be acceptable in our neighbors whose eyes are clouded with worldly things. We want YOU to look nice and advance in life. These are not reasonable curiosity in deep correct. As a matter of fact these are the most natural and beautiful things you could want. Just imagine a neighborhood that has people who love you and your children for who you are not what you have. You being a reflection of God. This is a life style that incorporates a loving community. It acknowledges you and your children to be beautiful regardless of what physical appearances seem to be. Better yet, a community that would not let a child feel inferior in any way. The community, by pooling resources would provide food, clothes, housing, schooling and a loving ergonomically safe environment to advance in life wonderfully in the light of God. This is Christ's way.

There are a few points that should be made before we go completely over the deep end. The first is that Christ told the rich official to sell everything and give it to the poor. The official could not do this, however, we know that many disciples did follow Christ's instruction but not all. This is also true now. Many of us are or will be called to sell every thing and follow Christ. Not everyone will be called to this type of life. However, everyone is called to be very, very careful about the value of their possessions. That fine line that defines a subjective degree of "rich" should not even be approached. As the person mentioned in the first paragraph of this article asked, "What right have we to acquire things beyond our needs while others haven't enough to eat?" That is a question that we must ask ourselves and be brutally honest about what we "need". If we can't leave this world not "needing" anything, we would easily ride that little camel.

Where is the major problem with this whole situation? Is it the misguided theory that Christ really did not mean what he said. Who perpetuates this theory? Those who wish to foster the increased reliance on worldly possessions as a barometer of true worth instead of God's light and the reflection of His love. Or might it be those who do not wish to alienate good friends, lose capitalistic competition, and face the rancor of the worldly people.

If we do not foster a Christian community attitude, we will never be able to truly follow Jesus Christ. Love is God's reflection in us. Love is sharing. Love can only be personified through our fellow human beings as "the Christ in front of us. It is impossible to live from a position of self indulgence, greed or unconcern. It is agreed that our love is effected by our position in life. It is also agreed that not all persons are called to give up everything. It is reasonable to lovingly care for ones family in modest circumstances and foster true community spirit. If all of us could create an atmosphere of non-excessive, non-competitive living conditions, the community of Christ would be an easily attained, as natural phenomenon.

We could then share our good fortune with those less fortunate according to their needs, without resentment.

Jesus states in JN 15: 17 "This I command you, Love One Another" If we love one another we will attain eternal unity with the Father. It seems that Jesus is saying that it is extremely difficult to be rich and love one another. He is not saying that it is impossible. (Frankly, I am still looking for that small camel.) Remember also that Christ reminds us that God can do what man sees as impossible. This means that we must rely on God for all of our earthly gifts, both physical and spiritual.

Reevaluating Christ's teaching and our position on the image of a rich person is not going to be easy. This action involves the fundamentally of everything. The principles that have been taught for years regarding the right to have what is called an affordable life.

How can we change this? Pray, honest evaluation of your material net worth, development of alternatives and affirmative action to allow us to be true Christians. Once you have gone through this procedure you will find that the "task is easy and the burden light".

Dear Grumps,

I am now a senior in high school and I have begun to look back on when I was younger, as a part of my life comes to an end. As I remember I realize that the thing that matters to me the most is family. The best times of my life so far have been with my family. I still fondly remember waiting at Aunt Colleen's house for you to arrive and upon singing we were rewarded with treats. The words "Grumps is great, he brings us chocolate cakes" still bring a smile to my face. In my mind as a young child you were amazing; it seemed to me that whenever you arrived, things always became more fun and exciting. You were life of things and the love that emanated from you was clear with every word you spoke. Even with the dim perception of a young boy I could easily tell that you were a great man and I admired you dearly because of it. Now when I see you with a more mature perspective on things, I see no difference. To me you are still the same amazing man that I knew as a child, or in the stories I had heard from my uncles and aunts. I just want to take the time on this Christmas to let you know how much you mean to me. So every time you see my picture I want you to always remember this; that no matter how old I get I will still see you as the unbreakable man with the heart of a lion, the only change is that you have now gained the wisdom that comes with time. So thank you for being you, and filling my life with love and warmth that will become memories that I will cherish for a lifetime.

Love,
Cory

A note from my Grandson

MY STARR

For reasons unknown In a family it's shown
With a wrath that is seeping To depth of it's own.
Without warning or fare it is suddenly there
And my Starr can do nothing But
Accept, with a hesitant flare.
"I have the disease but it doesn't have me "
He often declared with bravado,
a shield,
and to this daily dragon he refuses to yield.
With courage and hope he will accept
the results of a harsh education of exceptional length
In himself he found enough strength

To thwart the barbs and insults
that ignorance threw.
and survived every factor to diminish his stature
they only encourage his resolve to renew.

(This poem is about a young man who was stricken with
Huntington's Disease. His goal was to graduate from
high school. He did in his 21st year.)

THE SCHEME OF LIFE
"My View"

The pain was old with a familiar thrust
for years it reminded me of my bodily rust
If my regimen was not true
the pain would come thru
as a marathon finish I would pursue
the active less years were ten
and nightly walks were fairly slow
The pain returned when
Buck and I walked a mile or so

Poor bodily function was my thought
a nagging whisper hinted
that one might check on any pain
or have little to gain
by a dream to train
the discomfort away again.

This night the pain didn't go
to let me know all was not so

as it seems and relief was only a dream
call the Doc
use the clock
just to check the locks of my health and heart
time to depart from the world of schemes
(This poem was just prior to a quadruple bypass
surgery)

"AGAPE"

What would Jesus see
If He looked in a mirror,
Would He see Me?
Would he see a loving person? Without guile
Who has no need for cursing?
Or not returning a smile.
Would He see mercy, forgiveness and love,
or just me minding my own business.

He teaches us to love,
To let our neighbor live In peace
not from above,
But here were it's ours to give.
We are to show compassion
In our hearts and in our actions
To help avoid the world's attractions
and eliminate all non-loving factions.

Would He see the Christ I make up
With righteousness and force to take up
All the weapon we can wake up

To assure the world of daily shake up.

This shows our neighbor OUR God's mighty power
As interpreted through the mirror
We create, to be superior.
Would the image show a person who does know
That Christ's love must always show
Regardless of where we go.

Not for a minute, hour or day
But every NOWment in every way
In all we think or do or say
In everything, come what may.

We must try to be Christ's reflection
To strive to have His perfection
As a human, without rejection
And be His instrument of projection.

To be with our companions on this journey
 No violence in thought, word or action
To foster separation as a notion
To blur our true perception
Of what Christ's message is meant to be.
To turn away from a legal system
With justice instead of mercy
And turn to God's regal wisdom
To love all beings without diversity.

WHAT WOULD JESUS DO.......

If he was standing next to you
Would He use that "nasty" word
Or laugh when someone' s called a "nerd"
Would He patronize His mother
Or tell lies about his brother
Would He take money His dad "left around"
Or steal things and claim they were "found"

Would He walk away from a fight
Or always think that He was right
When He is afraid and feeling bad
Would He wish for things others had
Think of the things Jesus would do
With His love in your heart ask, would you?

You can change your whole personal view·
If you ask yourself "What Would Jesus Do"

9/11 UP SIDE DOWN

What would Jesus do with power,
if Mary, His mother, was in a Twin Tower In
His grief would He condemn?
Or would He love and forgive the men
Would He hunt down Ben Laden?
Or bomb where he has hidden.
His message is re-defined.

To allow murder of a different kind
Would He modify His commands
To justify a violent stand
Would He "in God trust" Or forget that we must
And not bring our version of "just"
Which allows beating Bin Laden to dust.
Jesus showed us so many ways
How to love our enemies in His last days
He forgave His killers with good intentions
And when He came back
Their names were not mentioned.

What would Jesus do I'm sure

Matt Corbliss, S.F.O.

He would never resort to war
Instead He would love His weakest of kin
Through forgiveness, understanding
And not discuss sin.

He would teach all God's people to follow the same
Loving path to our Father and His Holy Name.